HAPPY PLANNING

HAPPY PLANNING

Charlotte Plain

EBURY
PRESS

In loving memory of Dad, who always believed in me, who taught me to be myself and to find the positives in every situation. This book is dedicated to you for providing me with the happiest childhood memories that I will treasure forever.

Contents

Introduction

'A goal
without a plan
is just a wish'

Antoine de
Saint Exupéry

Welcome!

H i, I'm Charlotte – mum of three, dog-mum of two, wife to one, owner of Princess Planning and your new planning fairy godmother. And I am a woman on a mission – I want to let you in on my planning secrets. That's not so that you'll spend your life chained to yet another must-do list, but so that you can free up your time to do the things you love. For me, that means movie nights in with my kids, catch-ups with friends over tea and cake, and long baths with a glass of wine.

Planning your life can be anything from setting a monthly financial budget, compiling a weekly shopping list or arranging school holiday entertainment in advance, to a daily to-do or have-done list. In this book you will find the tools you need to take the pressure off your day-to-day through simple steps to help you get ahead. Forward thinking can be tough; it can be easy to fall into being reactive, manically responding to everyday crises with everything being a surprise. (Oh hey, did you book the kids in for half-term sports camp? Er … no. Did you remember to send Dad a birthday card? Whoops! Has the dog had his worm medication? Cue head-to-fist.) We all have so much to deal with that getting ahead of the mania (rather than being swept up in it) can seem like a pipedream. But when the pressure is on – organising childcare, functioning at work, navigating finances, resolving family disputes – simple things like budgeting and meal planning can keep the ship afloat.

It may seem daunting to implement such a system but it's easy, I promise, and I'll show you how.

I'm not saying planning will make everything perfect, but it will alleviate stress and help your budget, too. Thinking ahead about meals, life admin and upcoming events will instil a sense of control and boost confidence. You might initially think it frivolous or a hassle to allot a few minutes each day to planning, but you'll soon become hooked, because in the long run it will save you time.

For me, fitting in planning means getting up a little earlier in the morning when the house is quiet. Everyone's life follows a different rhythm, so I'll show you how to allocate some planning time each day that can be slotted in in various ways – for you, that might mean taking out your notebook on the train to work or making a list before bed each night. I find it wonderfully rewarding when I can tick off a few things from the to-do list – it gives me such a good feeling, and it better equips me for the inevitable challenges of the next day.

This book is broken up into three sections, so that you can plan for every day through keeping a food diary or devising a timetable to juggle work and family life; for special occasions like a birthday party or a wedding; and for bigger life events like moving house or finding a new job. Each section features my favourite tips for planning ahead as well as lots of practical ideas for making life run more smoothly (with an injection of fun too!). I'm going to hold your hand at every step and offer realistic tricks for those inevitable 'it's all gone to pot' moments!

Talking of 'going to pot', I wrote most of this book before the events of 2020 really took hold. With most of the 'normal' out of the window, I found that planning to keep on top of everything was so important for my physical and emotional wellbeing. Lists, trackers and my planning toolkit really kept me sane and healthy through lockdown – so I hope you'll find everything in this book even more relevant to keeping yourself happy.

I also want to get you thinking about your current habits and how they might be holding you back a bit, so at various points I will invite you to scribble down some thoughts, which means you'll need to have a pen and notebook at the ready (though if this isn't your bag, just skip these). You can read the book from start to finish or dip in and out of the chapters that speak to you, and by the end you'll be saying 'I can do this. I will do this!' despite everything that life is throwing at you.

It might surprise you, but I'm not a naturally organised person, however, I've taught myself the art of planning and forward thinking – that's right, organisation can be learned! So even if you've got an Olympic medal in procrastination with a fly-by-the-seat-of-your-pants character, fear not. You've got this.

My story

After many years as a stay-at-home mum the time came for me to return to work. I didn't know what the future would hold for me job-wise, but I started wondering if maybe I could turn my passion into my job. When I got married to Mr Princess Planning (aka Nick) a few years ago, I planned every aspect of the wedding, while at the same time lost several stone in the run-up to the big day. In order to do both, while also running a busy household, I needed to get organised. I started writing out my food plan for the week ahead, and I kept a daily diary, jotting down everything I was eating. It sounds so simple and obvious but just seeing the list really helped me keep on track and focus on my goal. Similarly, I wrote down thoughts, reminders and to-do lists for the wedding – scraps of paper became my life! All this forward planning, though, was what led to an amazing wedding day and a much trimmer me!

So it then occurred to me that I could try to make a business out of my love for order. After the kids went to bed one night I sat at my kitchen table and set about designing a food diary. I had no experience dreaming up artwork, so it was a real stab in the dark.

I wanted to design a food diary for busy women, like me, who were spinning plates and often forgot to prioritise themselves. The diaries would serve as a daily self-care reminder – even when time was really limited – to eat healthily and generally look after themselves. Time is our most precious commodity, so I knew most people would only have a couple of minutes a day free to fill it in and I needed to design something that was simple yet effective.

I had £600 in savings, but I took a leap of faith and ordered a DIY printing machine. I imagined I was my own customer, so I designed a package that appealed to me: a bright, sparkly cover with a motivational quote on the front that would boost confidence and inspire each owner. I started a little production line at home, with my kids helping, and I got printing – Princess Planning was born. Little did I know that within two years, having had no previous commercial experience whatsoever, it would become a business, sending out over 100,000 (and counting …) planning parcels a year. And thanks to my food diary – the first planner I created – I'm six stone lighter!

Why now?

Is it just me or does life feel busier than ever before? We're overloaded with work, parenting, endless housework, hobbies, kids' activities and neverending life admin. Enough already! We need a plan to get us out of this jam.

My approach to organisation isn't about being strict or admonishing ourselves when we haven't managed to juggle life perfectly. It's not about taking on even more life admin, in fact, quite the opposite. By adopting a few simple skills you can restore order to mayhem and look forward to events without dreading the extra work they involve. My approach can be applied to anything you need to plan – whether that's the everyday running of your household, a special event or even a major life change such as becoming a parent or switching jobs. Even if your planning issue is not covered in this book, you'll be able to apply these simple principles to nail it.

There's no point coming over all Monica from *Friends* and being efficient just for the sake of it so that we can pack more in and feel more rushed off our feet than ever. It's not about 'busy bragging' to our friends about how much we have on and are attempting to juggle. Instead, it's about saving time. I want you to reclaim those lost hours that you previously spent in a frazzled haze. So many of us are not just under pressure at home and at work, but every time we look on social media we are confronted with what looks like the perfect life – so far from our own reality where we're late for the school run, need two changes of clothes before 8 a.m. as the baby's been sick, have no milk in the fridge or no clean knickers.

And what I'd also like to give scope to is sometimes letting go of the plan. When life throws a curve ball and deviates our good intentions, that's okay. I have spent many years trying to let go of the ideal of perfection. I'd be fixated about having an impeccably tidy house or the kids turned out in the neatest school uniforms, and I'd feel rubbish when I inevitably couldn't achieve it. So while this book will help you implement a plan – be it for housework or starting your own business – it will hopefully also help you adapt when life laughs in the face of your plan.

Write it down

We are all motivated in different ways, but I've found that almost everyone I meet says they benefit from a sense of greater calm and focus after writing something down, be it a to-do list, a have-done list (i.e. a satisfying list all of the tasks they've already accomplished), their food choices or their worries. Sometimes these simple actions can have the most meaningful impact.

They can help us to visualise what we want to achieve, or give us an opportunity to reflect and to look forward.

Most of my customers tell me they are looking to create daily routines through putting pen to paper, with their wider view being to boost their wellbeing, improve their environment and generally make everything calmer. Having a little bit of me-time each day can massively impact on our overall happiness, so throughout the book I'll be giving you lots of reminders to factor it in. Self-care is an integral part of planning – if we're not looking after ourselves, how on earth can we look after others?

Some people swear by morning pages, where they scribble down their thoughts or to-do list for the day once they wake up in the morning. Others like to keep a notebook or planner by their bed so that before nodding off each evening they can jot down any worries or bullet points for the following day. For some, writing doesn't come easily and little sketches work better instead. For me, checking in with myself each day has become a routine – whether that's recording my daily food intake, writing a shopping list or taking a few minutes to think what I might do for myself (for more on self-care, go to page 86). I often feel a little lighter once I've scribbled down what's on my mind, like a weight has been lifted off my shoulders.

Does writing things down help you?

Tick which options below might help you squeeze in time for planning:

○   Early morning before anyone else is awake.

○   On your daily commute.

○   Having a five-minute tea break between tasks.

○   When the kids have gone to bed in the evening.

○   Just before you turn in, as the last thing you do before closing your eyes for the night.

Your planning toolkit

Whatever you're planning, whether it's your TV dinner or a wild hen-do weekend, my A, B, C, D, Es will help to get you focused and keep you focused. Give yourself as much time as possible – the longer you have to formulate a plan, the better. Don't jump in blindly, sit down and plan it properly when you have the time. Rushing a plan is arguably worse than having no plan!

A   Focus on the **aim** – what are you working towards? What are you trying to achieve? Keeping your eyes on the prize will sustain your motivation.

B   Nearly all plans involve a **budget** of some kind; crunch the numbers and make the figures work for you.

C   Surround yourself with good people and **communicate**. I always have more success when planning with my husband; for example, even a simple meal plan can fail if I didn't know that on Tuesday evening he is going to the match with the kids! This has a knock-on effect on both the budget and the shopping list.

D   No person is an island, so **delegate**. Family, friends and neighbours can all pitch in to make an event really special.

E   **Evaluate** and reassess your progress and pitfalls daily, weekly and monthly so that you can aim for continuous improvements. Think about what has worked well and what hasn't. How can the next day/week/month be better?

Now go forth and get planning!

Jot down your planning ideas here

....

....

....

....

....

....

....

....

....

....

....

....

....

....

....

....

....

....

One

Happy Planning Every Day

'Dream big, act fearlessly'

From managing your weekly shop, keeping an eye on your waistline and saving for a rainy day to bossing life admin, this section will make you the master of everyday drudgery. It will give you time back to do with whatever you want, whether that's learning Mandarin or lying on the sofa for a Netflix binge (you can guess which I'd prefer!).

Meals

Be the best version of you

I could almost write a whole book just about meal planning and the impact it's had on my life – from my journey with dieting, to family organisation and even to my business, where my meal planners are one of the most popular products.

Meal planning has turned my household around. It's also helped me shed a lot of weight – a total of six stone. I lost four stone before my wedding and it was in the run-up to the big day that I started recording my meals, writing down everything I'd eaten and drunk each day. I lost a further two stone after I got married, and I kept it off through continuing to plan meals.

It's not all about losing weight, though, there are so many benefits to meal planning. It can be a brilliant way to ensure you get a balanced diet full of nourishing foods, because we're all generally more considered when we think about meals in advance rather than buying on the spur of the moment for convenience. Having this sense of control rather than constantly chasing my tail in the kitchen eases the pressure when the kids come through the door shouting, 'What's for dinner?'. Consequently, we have little or no food waste and we've saved a lot of money through no longer duplicating ingredients or doing extra shopping trips in between (you know the ones – you nip to the supermarket for bread and milk and end up spending £30 on 'essentials'). I also find that if we do an order online from our list it's less tempting to add in treats, which are easy to grab off shelves impulsively when you're physically in a shop. Knowing what's on the menu also reduces the temptation to order a takeaway, meaning you'll keep the pounds in your purse, but not on your waist!

I'm going to let you into my simple formula for navigating mealtimes, which I keep in mind every day because it's been the secret to my six-stone weight loss. My **plan – shop – write – save** mantra forms the four pillars of my meal planning and I'm certain they'll help you too.

PLAN

Feel in control of my eating.

Focus on my goals.

SHOP

Work out the groceries we need for the weekly meal plan.

Compiling the shopping list as a family helps teach the kids about different ingredients and how to cook.

WRITE

Keep a daily food diary.

Have a weekly weigh-in, writing down the results.

Keeping track of your results helps you maintain a healthy weight.

SAVE

We spend less because we only buy what we need.

Food waste is reduced as we all eat the same meal.

We reduce calorie intake as we're making smarter food choices.

Shopping list

When I sit down with my family to meal plan we also compile a tear-off shopping list as we go as it saves time when you're in the supermarket or trawling online. Whether it's ingredients for our midweek breakfasts, daily snacks or our favourite Friday fakeaway, it all goes on the list.

In the past I would buy groceries, my husband would buy groceries, and we'd both get the same things without any idea of what we were trying to cobble together. Now every Sunday we sit down and decide what we are going to cook for every meal: breakfasts, lunches (both at home and on the go), dinners and snacks.

We look through the cupboard and fridge, see what's missing and compile a shopping list. We often flick through a recipe book while we're doing it to get a bit of inspiration, jotting down any ingredients we need. It's amazing the difference it's made to our overall time to spend just five minutes on a Sunday (or whatever day works for you!) gearing up for the week ahead. After several weeks of adopting this habit, it became a lot easier to budget for our weekly shop, too.

Here's my typical weekly shopping list of basics

Your Shopping List

MEAT AND FISH

FRUIT AND VEGETABLES

CUPBOARD

DAIRY AND FROZEN

HOUSEHOLD

ODD BITS

Your weekly meal plan

With a family of five, we aim for hearty, healthy meals, but even if we eat out, or have fish and chips at the weekend, we try to plan it in advance, writing it down on the family meal planner so that everybody knows what's on the menu and who's cooking. I've found that kids respond really well to forward planning and knowing what to expect. When they have a say in what we cook, it means we just make one meal rather than pandering to individual whims. By meal planning with them, they also know what their role will be when helping with the prep, such as peeling the potatoes. When filling in the meal plan, make a note if anyone won't be home for a particular meal to ensure nothing goes to waste (and your portions stay appropriate!).

Remember to keep your meal plans, then you can reuse them and make planning another week even easier. You can also scribble notes on them, adding a smiley face for the really popular meals.

Meal planning tips

We have worked these simple tricks into our routine as they are a massive help creating meals in minutes.

SLOW COOKING

We love our slow cooker as it's ideal for getting ahead on those nights when you know you won't have enough time to cook. Add your ingredients to the slow cooker in the morning and in the evening you'll be welcomed by an amazing smell of home-cooking. We use ours for meals like spag bol, campfire stew, chilli, casseroles and curries.

BATCH LOVE

If you have a large slow cooker or casserole, double up the ingredients when you cook and freeze half. Batch cooking saves so much time down the line as you can make several portions in one go, and you'll be glad of the ready-prepared meal on a busy day.

FOOD PREP

Every month or so, Nick or myself will try to spend a couple of hours in the kitchen with the radio turned up, prepping some ingredients for the freezer to make life easier. We might blitz up in the food processor a farm's worth of veg such as onions, garlic, celery and carrots, adding them to freezer bags so that they're chopped and ready to go on demand.

FREEZER JOY

Frozen homemade meals can be a real life-saver on those super-busy days. I buy containers from the pound shop and label them with the contents and date of freezing.

Weekly Meal Planner

DAY	BREAKFAST	LUNCH
___		
___		
___		
___		
___		
___		
___		

The menu planner we fill in each week — you could follow this or just write it all out on a blank sheet of paper if you prefer

DINNER

SNACK

Healthy weight loss

In two weeks, you'll feel it.
In four weeks, you'll see it.
In eight weeks, you'll hear it.

For some, planning meals is about getting organised, budgeting effectively and trying to creatively include a range of balanced food into meals for the family. For myself and a number of PP fans, it's all of those reasons as well as a way to keep track of any weight-loss goals. Losing weight isn't just about reducing your calorie intake, it's about helping to establish new habits and keeping them in place for the long term.

Like a lot of mums, I gained weight during my pregnancies, and although I managed to lose a little bit afterwards I never got to where I wanted to be.

My self-esteem had also taken a bit of a knock as the pounds piled on – I might be trying to do up a zipper that would no longer cooperate and started to wonder how has this happened? It kind of crept up and I really noticed it when doing simple things like chasing my toddler in the park or climbing the stairs. I'm sure I noticed it more than other people but it started consuming a lot of my headspace. I needed to bring a bit more control back when it came to my food choices so that I could feel more like my old self and stop stressing about it. Life's too short not to feel happy and well in yourself.

In fact, I would often make good progress only to revert to old habits again. As a result, I've tried every diet going (some more successful than others!) but it wasn't until I found Slimming World and became an online member that I could keep my weight on track. I was able to lose weight steadily but not miss out on eating hearty meals. When I combined the Slimming World approach with planning my meals and keeping a food diary, I got the greatest success ... allowing me to fit into my dream wedding dress. I find challenges really motivating, so 'slimming down for the gown' was something to aim for.

I weigh myself every Monday, recording what the scales tell me on my weight-loss chart and noting down any increases or decreases. I find this essential for keeping me on track and staying motivated. I often put on several pounds, particularly if I go on holiday or if we're having a celebratory birthday weekend, but I never worry too much about that because I know that once I start planning my meals again, I can get it back down. I'm a firm believer that we should all be able to indulge on special occasions!

My Weight-Loss Chart

lbs lost!

1lb	2lb	3lb	4lb	5lb	6lb	7lb	8lb
1lb	2lb	3lb	4lb	5lb	6lb	7lb	8lb
1lb	2lb	3lb	4lb	5lb	6lb	7lb	8lb
1lb	2lb	3lb	4lb	5lb	6lb	7lb	8lb
1lb	2lb	3lb	4lb	5lb	6lb	7lb	8lb
1lb	2lb	3lb	4lb	5lb	6lb	7lb	8lb
1lb	2lb	3lb	4lb	5lb	6lb	7lb	8lb

stones lost!

MY TREAT

9lb	10lb	11lb	12lb	13lb	*1*	
9lb	10lb	11lb	12lb	13lb	*2*	
9lb	10lb	11lb	12lb	13lb	*3*	
9lb	10lb	11lb	12lb	13lb	*4*	
9lb	10lb	11lb	12lb	13lb	*5*	
9lb	10lb	11lb	12lb	13lb	*6*	
9lb	10lb	11lb	12lb	13lb	*7*	

Food diary – if you bite it, you write it

It can be really hard to make smart choices when we're tired after a long day. Is there anything more dangerous than a post-work supermarket dash when you're hungry and not quite sure what it is you're looking to buy? That's certainly when I used to grab for the ready meals or a salty, fat-laden snack for the commute home.

I've always loved food, big portions and the ritual of mealtimes. I come from a family where there was always a delicious home-cooked roast dinner on the table, where the portions were massive and we always finished with a pudding. It was wonderful and gave me a real appreciation of sitting down together as a family at mealtimes, but it did mean having to re-evaluate things like portion sizes when I started having an honest look at my weight.

I've already told you that wanting to fit into my dream wedding dress was my goal, and although I was able to achieve this with the help of following Slimming World, perhaps the most important factor was writing down what I was eating and planning my meals. It made me realise that taking just a few minutes out of my day to record what I was eating and snacking on was the secret. Since starting Princess Planning, I've been trying to get the message out about this so that I can help other people just like me.

Another trick I rely on is to keep a list of my favourite treats along with their Slimming World 'Syns' as a go-to page in my planner. (If you've not done Slimming World, Syns are treats/snacks that have a calculated synergy value, which you can have a certain amount of each day.) Doing this means I can refer to them and make a choice depending on the day in the full knowledge of what they're worth. I have found that this really helps me stay on track. If you don't use Syns, you could use calories instead or the Weight Watchers points system.

My Favourite Treats

Caramel Freddo	Kinder snack bar
Freddo	Mini Crunchie
10 Cal Jelly	Meringue nest
Options Hot Chocolate	White Lion bar
Mini Party Rings	Mini Skittles
Pink 'n' Whites	Trio
Fibre One Cake Bar	Curly Wurly
Chewits pack	Viscount mint biscuit
Jaffa Cake	Lovehearts
Mikado Sticks	Fudge
Digestive Thins	Flumps
Creme Egg	Chomp
Milky Bar	Raspberry ripple

My Before and After Food Diary

TYPICAL MEALS BEFORE WEIGHT LOSS	TYPICAL MEALS NOW
BREAKFAST Cereal with milk	**BREAKFAST** Overnight oats
LUNCH Pasty and cake	**LUNCH** Ham, cheese and salad with pitta bread
DINNER Lasagne with garlic bread	**DINNER** Chilli and rice
SNACKS Crisps Chocolate	**SNACKS** Small chocolate treats Yoghurt Fruit

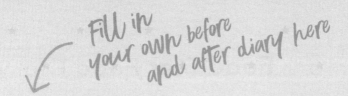
Fill in your own before and after diary here

TYPICAL MEALS BEFORE WEIGHT LOSS	TYPICAL MEALS NOW
BREAKFAST	**BREAKFAST**
LUNCH	**LUNCH**
DINNER	**DINNER**
SNACKS	**SNACKS**

Food Diary

	BREAKFAST	LUNCH	DINNER
MON			
TUES			
WED			
THURS			
FRI			
SAT			
SUN			

Wake up with determination, go to bed with satisfaction

SNACKS

GOALS

I aim to lose

_____ this week!

This week's results

_____ !

Staying on track

If you've started planning your meals and/or are keeping a food diary, you might like to take a few minutes each day to write down any thoughts, progress made or setbacks – I often find this helps me to keep looking forward.

✳ Write down your goals for the coming week, month and year. Revisit them often to have an honest check-in about progress.

✳ If I need a bit of a back-to-basics reset, I reread my Slimming World recipe books, pretending it's my first ever week. This helps me garner enthusiasm.

✳ Emotions around food and eating can be complicated, and if you are embarking on this new food plan, it might bring up mixed emotions. Thinking about our food associations can really shed light on our eating habits and that in turn can help with your planning success.

✳ Record any achievements – and I don't just mean a reduction on the scales. It might be that you've made a healthier food choice where previously you wouldn't have, drunk more water, reduced food waste or done some exercise – it all counts and it's all amazing!

✳ Remember that the most important thing is to feel well in yourself, and that looks different for all of us. Your mental health and wellbeing should always come before dieting. It's not about comparing ourselves to others – look to your own achievements and goals.

Use this page to jot down your motivations
for staying on track and feeling good

....

....

....

....

....

....

....

....

....

....

....

....

....

....

....

....

Budgeting

Don't give up what you want most for what you want now

Managing your finances is a skill and has very little to do with how much you earn. Money worries can creep into all aspects of our lives, casting a shadow on our enjoyment of simple things as anxiety mounts. It's so tempting to bury our heads in the sand and ignore mounting debt or be convinced that we *need* a new dress, car or even a home. But having a handle on our expenditure is motivating, after all, making a plan is saying 'I can'! The relief I have felt after writing down a rough plan is almost physical – like a heavy weight lifting off my shoulders. Bringing control back into your decision-making around money is the first step to good financial planning. Having a plan to follow and check back in with if you fear you are veering off course takes away much of the pressure and day-to-day decision-making. It may seem rigid and counterintuitive, but having a plan is liberating. It will help you to look ahead with optimism and leave behind any spending shame.

Have you ever bought something new where you initially felt exhilarated, only to then feel a bit guilty and unsettled? I know I have. Social media has a lot to answer for when it comes to making us insecure. Influencers often get paid thousands of pounds to advertise products in a post, sometimes leaving us feeling not quite good enough, even if we don't know why.

A friend of mine got into real trouble with gambling, which started out as a £10 bet on a football match but then spiralled out of control. Loan after loan was maxed out as he couldn't stop himself placing bets on any sporting fixture he could think of, even obscure ones he previously had no interest in. He soon started feeling like there was no way out, and the effect on his family life was so sad to see. This is an extreme case but unfortunately one that is pretty common. Money can be a hugely emotional topic, and anxiety around it can be detrimental not only to our mental health but also to our relationships and the wellbeing of the whole family. We all want to live the best life we can while staying out of the red.

On the following pages I've listed some simple steps so that you can take action today to sort out your finances. Soon you'll start to spend money with your head, not your heart.

Set a realistic budget within which you can live

Budgeting is arguably the most important job for any household, but in my experience it is one that is done infrequently. Following a budget takes organisation and relies on careful planning.

When budgeting, keep your goal(s) in mind. What are you hoping to achieve? Do you want to put money away for a rainy day? Move to a bigger house? Be able to indulge a little at birthdays? Or do you simply want to have more free time, created by being able to say no to taking on extra work to keep afloat? Maybe you just want to feel more in control of your outgoings? Priorities will change at different stages of life but budgeting will likely be crucial no matter what the phase. Write down your current goals for budgeting and pin this list somewhere visible in your home, such as on the fridge or your dressing table.

I'm a strong believer in sitting down with your partner (if you have one) or just by yourself to examine your finances in a totally honest way. Getting the basics down on paper is beneficial as visual cues can really give us a reality check.

✳ Calculate your total monthly income, including salary or benefits such as income support and child benefit.

✳ List every outgoing, including set expenses such as rent/mortgage, car payments, insurance, loans, nursery fees, phone and credit card payments.

✳ List your variable expenses, such as clothing, food, fuel and utilities. This will be an estimate and, if in doubt, round it up rather than down.

* List your non-essential expenses, such as eating out, nights out, hobbies, charity donations and holidays. Get the calendar out in front of you so that you can see whether any birthdays are coming up or any other events that you'll need to shell out for.

* Total it all up! Hopefully you'll be in the black and have the opportunity to save a little money each month. If not, you will need to make cuts, and the best place to start is with your non-essentials (more on this on page 42).

* Set up different bank accounts for different things, such as back-to-school funds or holiday savings. You'll be less likely to dip into these provisions if they're separate to your regular current account.

Just by writing all this down, you may feel a release. Follow your budget as closely as you can and add, change or re-evaluate on a month-to-month basis. Of course, feel free to tweak my budget planner to make it personal to your circumstances.

>>> *Turn over to see the budget template I use to keep track, which you can fill in here or on a sheet of paper*

Expenses Tracker

MONTH ....

DATE	DESCRIPTION	IN	OUT

TOTAL IN	TOTAL OUT	BALANCE

Budget Tracker

MONTHLY SALARY	EXTRA INCOME	TOTAL INCOME

EXPENSES	BUDGETED	ACTUAL	DIFFERENCE
Set			
Variable			
Non-essential			

Final Balance	

Cutting costs

It can be difficult to increase our monthly income (if only it were easy!), but something you do have some control over is spending. A really effective method that I have to shave money off our essential monthly payments is to use a comparison website to get the best deals available. I went through the list below and was able to make savings on most of them. Even if sometimes it is just a few pounds on each, it really does add up.

Home insurance
Electricity
Gas
TV subscriptions
Internet
Mobile phones
Car insurance
Credit card interest
Gym membership

The benefit of analysing honestly your weekly and monthly expenditure is that it sometimes becomes obvious where you are splurging, often mindlessly. When we sat down to look at ours, we spotted the daily transaction of my husband's café-bought coffee – the £3 a day added up to £15 a week, totalling a massive £780 a year! It really is alarming once you think of those few pounds a day in terms of the bigger picture. Needless to say, he started packing a flask of coffee each morning and now puts the £15 a week into our holiday account.

Some banks allow you to track your spending by breaking it down into different categories to show you where you're spending the most, and you can then set budgets accordingly to prevent overspending. There are also banks and apps where you can opt into a micro-saving scheme whereby whenever you spend money, e.g. £1.80, the change (20p) goes into your savings account automatically. It's a digital version of the change pot you might keep at home.

Ditching the debt

The thrill of 'buy now, pay later', where you don't see the transaction on your bank statement immediately, can make it all too easy to spend, and stores know this. But spending doesn't necessarily mean owning. Aggressive marketing tells us we need that bag/sofa/cute kid's outfit NOW. Tapping into comparison culture and our insecurities, brands are experts at promoting FOMO. Spending can give an instant hit of endorphins, giving us a little high perhaps when we're feeling low. For some, spending is also linked to self-esteem and how we try to deal with complicated emotions. Supermarkets and even online shops have developed sophisticated methods of luring us in, convincing us to buy products we didn't even know we needed. In a society where we are constantly being advertised to, it can be hard to approach spending in a measured way. With this in mind, I've found it essential to plan my purchases in advance, so that I'm following my head and not my heart. That's where the 'non-essential spending' section of my budget tracker comes in. Putting money aside for treats means that I may need to save up for a coat I've had my eye on, but if I do buy it, it's a really considered purchase. I am a big advocate of working hard and spending my money, guilt-free, on what I actually want, rather than what I'm told I want. Best of all, that hard-earned cash could be saved for an experience such as a day out with the kids – something you'll remember for years to come.

As I've said, writing down all of your incoming and outgoing funds, and honestly assessing them, is essential for mapping out your present and future budget.

To keep track of my progress I find it helpful to:

✳ Check my balance every day across my accounts.

✳ Go through my online bank statement to make sure there are no irregularities (such as being charged twice for the same transaction, which isn't uncommon).

✳ Reduce my spending where possible (buying supermarket 'essential' brands is one way to tighten the belt).

✳ Always go shopping with a list, otherwise I am susceptible to veering off course and over-spending.

✳ Freeze credit card spending.

✳ Sell on eBay or Depop anything around the house that we're no longer using, such as clothes and old toys.

Saving money

I was a stay-at-home mum before launching Princess Planning, so money was particularly tight.

Even now, we are always looking at how to save, and one way we've managed to set aside little amounts every week is to have a few separate bank accounts, such as:

* Current account for day-to-day expenses, such as rent/mortgage, bills and groceries.

* Holiday account to ease the pressure when we want to book a trip.

* Emergency account to cover unexpected events, such as car repairs or the boiler breaking.

* Celebration account to cover things like birthday gifts and Christmas.

* Rainy day savings account for longer-term goals, such as the kids' university fees.

* Children's accounts: I set up ISA accounts for all three of my children when they were born, to which we add a little each month. At seventeen, they will be able to access these funds themselves to use them to help with something like buying a car. My family have also been adding to them over the years in lieu of birthday and Christmas gifts.

Though it's so satisfying to see the numbers in your savings account creep up (and debt creeping down), saving can feel gruelling at times. It can seem like everyone else is having the best time splashing the cash, especially when you look at the fantasy world portrayed by social media. I try to be grateful for what I have rather than looking at what others are doing.

Happiness in life is found in the simple things, and here are a list of my favourite things to do that cost little to nothing:

* Going for a walk while listening to a podcast.

* Reading a book curled up in my favourite chair, with a hot choc in hand.

* Baking with the kids, letting them get messy, then enjoying the tasty rewards.

* A movie night at home with the whole family squeezed onto the sofa.

* Visiting a free museum for a little culture hit.

* Making a picnic at home and taking it to the park.

Have short-, medium- and long-term goals when it comes to your finances

If you are always finding yourself trying to eke out the last of your pay each week or month, you'll know how stressful that can feel. Having a goal can be really motivating, helping you stick to your plan.

Write down what you'd do if you were spending your nest egg today:

....

....

....

....

....

....

What would you do with it in two years?

....

....

....

....

....

How about in fifteen years?

If you are saving up for something in particular, whether it's a pair of shoes or a wedding, it can be really inspiring to create a vision board, popping it somewhere visible at home to help you keep your eyes on the prize. On it you could have a mix of photos, magazine cut-outs, positive words and affirmations (such as the ones at the start of this section). This can serve as a great way to set goals and prioritise your spending (especially when your head is turned by something else to buy).

Teaching kids about budget planning

I'm sure all parents have been there – you're at the shops and your child sees a toy they absolutely *need* right now! Their birthday was last month and Christmas is ages away. They start getting upset when you tell them they can't have it and soon you're getting looks from other shoppers. If this sounds familiar, maybe it's time to get your kids to start planning too? Whether it's saving up pocket money in return for doing small tasks at home or keeping a wish list of things they see that they want, it can help a child to learn the value of money as well as how to choose carefully when spending it. I try not to shut down conversations with my kids around things that they want. Instead, I might explain how it's not possible to buy it right now but that we can work out a plan for how to save for it. If the item in question is important to them (rather than something they've just seen in passing), it may take months or longer of saving to get it, making it extra special when they do.

Budgeting is such an important life skill I'm surprised more time isn't spent on it at school. These days, kids may not even see much cash change hands, they're so used to observing transactions made with the swipe of a card, so there might be a disconnect in their minds about how money actually works. So, for me, it's even more important to try to set an example at home. My kids see my husband and I discussing money in an open, relaxed way.

Here's a children's budget that kids from about the age of ten upwards might want to fill in. It's a pared-back version of the one I use and it's meant to be an accessible and fun opportunity for them to get into the habit of budgeting.

Children's Budget Tracker

POCKET MONEY	EXTRAS	TOTAL INCOME

EXPENSES	BUDGETED	ACTUAL	DIFFERENCE
Set			
Variable			
Non-essential			

Final Balance	

Yay!

Whether you're saving a couple of pounds on your weekly shop, adding to your holiday fund or resisting that dress you didn't really need, managing to run your life and possibly a household while paying the bills and perhaps putting a little extra aside is no mean feat. Know that with a good plan, you will be able to approach your finances differently and feel in control.

Recognise any achievements here, big or small ...

....

....

....

....

....

....

....

....

....

....

Home life

I do what I can, when I can.

Housework can be the bane of our existence. With three kids and a hectic business, I have at times struggled to keep on top of it. We live in a small–medium house and with two beagles thrown into the mix (who are only allowed downstairs!), plus me sometimes working from home, the space is worked pretty hard. I'm lucky that my husband, Nick, is naturally very tidy and organised (more so than I am …) so together we approach our home as a team planning exercise. I'm a huge believer in sharing jobs among the whole family (more on this to come) – my husband and I do the majority but help from the kids lessens the load. I am someone who is affected by the space around me so it's good for my well-being to have everything more or less in order in my home. I find it disheartening to come home after a long day to find the place in disarray, so everything being in its place brings me a sense of calm.

Daily habits

For some, the mere sight of an unwashed cup in the sink will give an unsettling feeling, while for others mess is invisible. You'll have heard myriad approaches to housework, from those who recommend doing a bit every day to those who suggest doing a full blowout once a week and then being housework-free the other six days. The problem with the latter approach is that there tends to be more to do when you're not chipping away at it every day, meaning you actually spend more time on cleaning overall.

Little and often is our housework mantra. I don't want to be spending precious hours over the weekend with a cloth in my hand. Similarly, I try to tackle it first thing in the morning, getting up before the kids so that I can tick off a few jobs before we leave for work, so that our evenings aren't taken up with it. Nobody has time to clean a house top to bottom every day, so evaluating what time I have daily, on which days I may have more time and which jobs need doing is vital. And, you've guessed it, I plan this all out in advance, creating a family weekly rota, which I rally the whole household to buy into and take responsibility for.

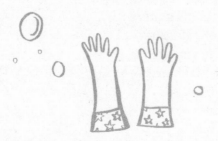

Household jobs

First things first, let's assess what needs doing. Here's my go-to list of household jobs:

DAILY: Wash up, empty the dishwasher, clean kitchen surfaces, light vacuum/sweep and mop of kitchen floors, make beds, put on one load of laundry, clean loo, wipe down bathroom surfaces.

WEEKLY: Dust, mop floors, vacuum, iron, change bedsheets and towels, take out the bins, clean smear marks off mirrors, glass and kitchen cabinets, shake out rugs and animal bedding if you have any pets (and vacuum up debris), wipe down fridge trays, clear out coat and shoes space (which if it is anything like mine is overflowing after a day, with clothing that could be kept up in bedrooms), thorough clean of the bathroom, mopping the floor.

1–3 MONTHS (depending on how fastidious you are): Clean win-dows, a deep clean of the fridge and its compartments, clean oven, wash out bins, wipe down door knobs and light switches, clean scuff marks off walls, wash cushion covers and sofa covers (if removable), clean out the filters of devices such as the washing machine, dishwasher and extractor fan.

QUARTERLY: Clean out drawers or cabinets around the house, remove any junk that's built up, such as chargers, post or old batteries, and either bin them or restore them to their rightful place; give your home a more thorough dusting than the weekly one, including behind the radiators and along skirting boards that are more out of reach, such as the ones under the bed; clean out kitchen cabinets to remove dust and dirt.

Cleaning Chores

DAILY TASKS

....

....

....

....

....

....

....

Monday ⚪ ⚪

Tuesday ⚪ ⚪

Wednesday ⚪ ⚪

Thursday ⚪ ⚪

Friday ⚪ ⚪

Saturday ⚪ ⚪

Sunday ⚪ ⚪

WEEKLY TASKS

....

....

....

....

....

....

....

1–3 MONTHS

QUARTERLY

Your family weekly rota

In my home, the weekly rota keeps us all in check. When we created the rota we all sat down together to decide as a team who was going to take on which chores. I've found there's less resistance this way, rather than doling out jobs and feeling like a manager in my own home. It also means that people can play to their strengths and not take on chores they really despise. Every member of the family is on there, as well as the list of jobs we're all allocated. This does not need to change every week, in fact it's simplest if it doesn't. There are apps that can help with this but I find the old-fashioned way works well, especially as our rota is in our kitchen and so not easy to miss. If you follow this plan every week, it soon becomes second nature and the kids don't need to be chased up (most of the time!). If you have small children, they may find stickers a fun way to stay motivated.

I'm always surprised at how much I can get done in five minutes, especially when I'm listening to the radio.

To give a sense of timing, here's what we get done in our home in short to longer bursts:

ABOUT 5 MINUTES: Making the bed and doing a quick mine-sweep of the bedroom, putting away any stray items of clothing, toiletries, books, etc.; gathering up clothes from laundry baskets and sticking on a wash (I sometimes use the timer setting on the washing machine so that it switches on in the early hours and then I can hang out the clothes to dry as soon as I get up in the morning); washing up of breakfast dishes, cleaning of the loo and wipe-down of the bathroom surfaces; cleaning out our dogs' beds and food/water bowls.

15 MINUTES: Light vacuum of the whole downstairs and a mop of the kitchen floor.

30 MINUTES: Deep clean of the bathroom.

1 HOUR: Cleaning the oven.

If, for example, I only have 10 minutes before a friend pops round, I grab an empty basket or box and charge around the house throwing everything in my path into it. I'll then quickly wipe down the bathroom surfaces, including the loo, making sure there's loo roll and a clean, dry towel hanging up. I always remember how I feel when stopping by a friend's house, particularly when it's an unexpected visit. Do I expect it to be gleaming with every little object in its perfect place, fresh flowers on the table and a batch of scones baking in the oven? Actually, I think I'd find that more unnerving than the morning's washing up still in the sink and the post lying on the hallway floor!

Family Weekly Rota

NAME		
MONDAY		
TUESDAY		
WEDNESDAY		
THURSDAY		
FRIDAY		
SATURDAY		
SUNDAY		

Use this as a family to keep track of your chores throughout the week.

Make it easy for yourself

Keep all your cleaning products in an accessible place. Using a caddy for products is handy because it means I can just grab the whole thing from under the sink and take it around with me, cleaning as I go. If I had to look in different cupboards for a cloth and various detergents every time, I think I'd fall at the first hurdle. The same goes for vacuum cleaners – the cordless ones make the process a lot easier than lugging a big one around the house, the flex getting tangled and me huffing and puffing. I know people who have an automated robot vacuum, which goes about its business while its owner has its feet up – sounds appealing!

Adjusting our mindset

This is where applying a bit of a 'fake it 'til you make it' mindset comes in. I try to view housework less as a chore and more as a ritual of care for my home. I know, I know, sounds a bit out-there, but stay with me.

There are some religious orders who see housework as much about cleansing your home as cleansing your mind. Starting in the morning with a little sweep of the floors while thinking about the day ahead – or better yet, not thinking about anything much at all – offers us a chance to nurture our environments. Okay, I know it's not quite a champagne breakfast in bed, which is frankly how I'd probably choose to start my day, but trying not to associate housework with being a burden has helped me a little.

Housework and kids

For me, there's a balance between letting the kids get messy, having free rein to be creative and uninhibited and teaching them a bit about looking after our environment. I try not to be too precious during playtime – young children need space to play and to let their imaginations run wild. If you popped by my house on any given afternoon, particularly a few years ago when my kids were smaller, you'd likely find Lego all over the floor, marker pens under the sofa and books pulled off the shelf half-read. I like to give my kids freedom of expression without hovering over them, micro-managing their every move.

Having said all that, I do feel it's important for kids to take responsibility for their belongings as well as to contribute to the general wellbeing of the home. Even if it's just keeping their rooms clean and tidy, every bit helps.

Children watch everything we do, and instilling good habits from an early age can help to set these up for life. The idea that the child is part of a family where everyone pitches in gives them a sense of ownership and responsibility. And most of the time young children love to 'help' – okay, we may need to adjust our expectations here, it's unlikely you'll have your toddler cleaning the windows, but there's still plenty they can do with your encouragement! This approach has worked in our home and actually I think has helped my eldest son when he joined the Royal Navy, where everything has to be ... shipshape (ahem!).

Tasks (even young) children can help with

Tidying up at the end of the day: putting away one set of toys before starting with another.

Hanging up their coats (on a reachable hook) and putting their shoes away.

Making their bed each morning.

Sweeping the floor.

Putting clothes away in cupboards or a laundry basket.

Helping with meal prep, such as washing fruit and veg.

Laying the table.

Fill in with your own

Tips for dealing with kids' belongings

If possible, have toys grouped together in a little box, basket, shelf or tray, in an accessible place where your child can access them without your help. Keep a basket in the hallway or at the bottom of the stairs. Before the bedtime wind-down begins, do a clear-up of your home (ask your kids to join in!), gathering everything into the box, then on the way up to bed, ask each child to collect what's theirs and put it away. If you do this every evening, this little ritual will begin engrained and you won't even have to ask anymore. It then means that when you come downstairs after their bedtime, you'll be greeted with a less cluttered space, which is welcome if you've just spent the previous hour wrangling your kids into bed.

Spring clean

I'm not going to tell you to throw away everything you own –
we've heard enough of that. Though I must admit I have found
having a bit of a clear-out not only practical in a home but also
therapeutic, even when I'm just spending a few minutes tidying
up a drawer in the kitchen (which mysteriously always ends up
full of elastic bands and takeaway menus). For children, a one-in
one-out rule can be an essential guideline for limiting the sheer
volume of stuff they have. Obviously, if you have the luxury of
large children's bedrooms or even a separate playroom, you can
be less strict about this.

When it comes to clothes, most of us wear just a small proportion
of what's in our closets – I am definitely guilty of choosing my old
favourites every day, meaning that the cost per wear of some of
my outfits, particularly some of my 'occasion' dresses, is enough
to make my eyes water! To keep the clothes jumble under control,
I hang everything up in the order in which I wear them, so, for
example, this evening I'll hang up the jeans I'm wearing on the
far left of the rail. If you do the same, you'll be able to see really
easily what you're actually using and the right-hand side of the
rail will likely be full of things you wear infrequently. Ask yourself
if realistically you're going to wear them – are they worth the
space they're taking up? If you're not sure (and I often have this
problem, especially if the item of clothing was pricey), pop a small
box at the bottom of your wardrobe or beside your chest of drawers
and throw in there anything you can't make up your mind about.
Look in the box after a few weeks and see how you feel – have you
missed anything in there? Is there anything you want to pull out
and wear immediately? If not, maybe it's time to say goodbye.

Every six months or so, I rally the whole family to spend an hour in their bedrooms making a pile in the middle of the floor of stuff they no longer need. Clothes, toys and books then get rounded up for the charity shop. Selling online on eBay or Depop is another great option for recouping costs and it always feels like free money!

As much as it might be easier if I just blitzed the children's rooms every few months, clearing out things I know they no longer use, I draw the line at throwing away other people's belongings (it's not easy to resist the urge to blowtorch some of the kids' mangy 'well-loved' toys, let me tell you!). In the past when I have bagged up old toys for charity that my kids haven't played with in ages, they start rummaging through them declaring their undying devotion to them and plead with me to keep them – it's a question of either saying yes or having the toy surgically removed from their hands! So I find it much more effective if everyone just does their bit. Keeping it to a short chunk of time, putting on some music (and perhaps having a treat to look forward to afterwards!) does the trick. And the less stuff we have, the less there is to clean.

Let it go

For those of us who struggle with perfectionism, keeping on top of household chores can be such a challenge, and when it inevitably doesn't happen from time to time, we can feel really demoralised. When our self-worth is tied into our productivity, it's like we're setting ourselves up for a fall. That to-do list feels like a mountain; we can never seem to get to the bottom of it without more being added on. And let's face it – no matter how effective we are at planning, there's always going to be something else to do, isn't there? That thought alone can be really overwhelming. There will be some days, weeks or months when you won't be able to keep all those balls in the air and pure survival becomes the priority. The bedsheets go unchanged, the floor unmopped and everyone may be eating cereal for dinner. And that's okay, because during times like this, we just need to keep on keeping on. Let go of the plan a little and do what you need to do. We're all doing the best we can and when circumstances settle down, order will be restored. After all, on your death bed are you going to look back on life and think, 'I really wish I'd dusted more?'

Family life

Small steps every day

Establishing routines at home can help children thrive – it's never too early to bring them into the planning zone!

Children go through so many phases and the weeks/months over which these are happening can feel like a lifetime. I have found that the teenage years were definitely the hardest for me. It was a time of real transition, when my older two felt like adults themselves and wanted to be treated as such but really they still had so much to learn. I've found having predictable routines really help children to feel settled, from babyhood all the way through to their teens.

Something I have tried to instil in my children from an early age is the need for them to plan their day-to-day, whether that's to do school work, have fun with friends or schedule time together as a family. Managing their own time, rather than me or my husband barking at them, helps them learn the vital organisational skills they will need in adult life and means they can prioritise what they want to do, too. As part of this our kids all have a level of responsibility at home, with daily jobs they must carry out, such as feeding the dogs or helping with shopping or preparing meals. Families need to act as teams with everyone contributing something so that one individual isn't over-burdened.

Life isn't perfect and anyone who lives with a teenager will know there are ups and downs, with emotions often running high. I always remind myself that they're developing so much, both mentally and physically, and that kindness and positivity can go a long way to supporting them. Keeping their spirits up, boosting their confidence and reminding them that tomorrow is a new day is sometimes all we can do to keep life on course.

Daily routines

I believe that routines and knowing what to expect each day help make a child feel secure, whatever their age.

REUBIN (aged nine)

MORNING	AFTER SCHOOL
Wake.	Activity, such as boxing, swimming, football or cricket.
Eat breakfast.	Help with dinner prep.
Brush teeth.	Eat dinner with family.
Get dressed.	Play on iPad or Xbox (for no longer than 30–40 minutes).
Make bed, folding pyjamas under pillow.	Prepare school bag ready for the next day.
Quick tidy of bedroom, putting away anything on the floor.	Spellings and reading time (20 minutes each).
Get school bag, put on coat and shoes.	Pop clothes away and tidy any other bits in bedroom.
	Shower, pyjamas on and brush teeth.
	Hop into bed, lights out.
	Sleep.

Happy Planning

Here are the rhythms my children follow Monday – Friday during Term-time.

HARRIET (teenager)

MORNING

Wake.

Have a big glass of water and eat breakfast.

Feed pets.

Brush teeth /skincare.

Get dressed.

Make bed.

Quick tidy of bedroom.

Phone time (no more than 20 minutes).

Get school bag ready, and coat and shoes on.

AFTER SCHOOL

Eat a snack whilst having phone time (about 20 minutes).

Do homework.

Eat dinner with family.

Shower, pyjamas and brush teeth.

Make sure bag and clothes are ready for next day.

Watch TV or read a book in bed.

Sleep.

Term-time topsy-turvy

On page 165 I share with you some strategies to battle school holidays, but what about term-time chaos, where you're in the thick of the Monday–Friday grind? We know it takes a village to raise a child, but if you're living nowhere near family, you'll need to create your own village. Having some backup can make the world of difference, both practically and psychologically.

* Share your pick-ups and drop-offs if you can. If you have a partner or a pal, try to divide it up fairly. If you're a single parent, can you put a message out about sharing? Taking five minutes to chat or message could save you lots of time in the future. Remember to let the school know if someone else will be picking up your child.

* Have a shared calendar, either digitally or put it up somewhere that everyone can see it. That way, everyone can check who is where and what they are meant to be doing.

* Build in a contingency time for the school run of 10 minutes, aiming to leave earlier for the inevitable did-I-shut-the-front-door/I-am-still-wearing-my-slippers? scenarios.

* If a breakfast club sounds appealing but your school doesn't have one, could you create a DIY one, taking it in turns with likeminded parents and reciprocating once a week?

* Start a babysitting club with friends or neighbours so that you can have a well-deserved evening out and then return the favour for friends, thus avoiding the hassle and expense of finding a trustworthy babysitter.

Make the mornings relaxed and the evenings energised

Think of your mornings as they are now. I presume they're as serene as a health spa, everyone unruffled, happy worker bees doing their thing. Lol! I can't say mine are always calm but we have established a few tricks at home to help them flow better. It's not rocket science, but we try to get as much prepared the night before as we can. Coats and school bags are hung on their hooks and ready to go. PE kit is packed. My husband's flask is on the counter waiting to be filled with coffee. Phones are left downstairs to charge overnight. Everyone is responsible for their own belongings. These small actions can save your patience in the morning and prevent you losing your rag before 7.30 a.m. (not a great precedent for the day ahead!). If I have time, I lay out breakfast bowls and cups, and even make breakfast the night before.

Think about the route from your busy area (probably the kitchen) to the front door or car. Is it a minefield of detritus such as lost homework, junk mail or random shoes? This will make it harder to get out each morning and in turn increase the argy-bargy ('We're going to be late AGAIN!').

Let kids learn to do things for themselves. This was a hard one for me as, let's face it, it's quicker to help a small child put their coat on than letting them do it themselves – all fingers and thumbs while they stop to have a five-minute daydream about a button. But the more they do it, the quicker they'll get, leaving one less thing for you to do.

Family Weekly Calendar

NAME		
MONDAY		
TUESDAY		
WEDNESDAY		
THURSDAY		
FRIDAY		
SATURDAY		
SUNDAY		

Keep your family organised:
list each member's activities for the week
— not just for kids but grown-ups too!

The dreaded H-word

The kids are back from school, they rush in, taking off their bags and coats, carefully hanging them up in their rightful place. They've had a super day of education and they can't wait to tell you all about the facts they learnt in history. They're desperate to start their maths homework so they scamper to their room while you have a much-deserved cuppa. Okay, maybe not. More likely, they return tired and hungry as they slump on the sofa and demand a snack.

It can be so hard to motivate kids with homework or other chores without sounding like a nagging dragon. My kids know that we value the importance of school and we encourage them to take responsibility for their workload. When it comes to homework, some days it is easier than others to encourage them to do it. On tougher evenings, I find it helps to give them a choice, a bit of carrot and stick – get it done now and have it out of the way or have a little rest and make a start in half an hour when they're more relaxed. You might offer the kitchen table or the little desk in their bedroom, along with a piece of toast or apple slices to soften the blow. And so on.

Get real

There will be some days you're foaming at the mouth in irritation. Kids, young kids especially, don't care about mess, your need to be on the 8.12 a.m. to Doncaster or Dad missing the start of his shift. And actually, it's good that their little brains aren't getting worried about these more humdrum aspects of life (maybe we could all benefit from being in the moment like they are?). When I'm at my wits' end with one of my lot, I try to remind myself to breathe – in for four, out for eight – and I remember our priorities are different.

And then I scream into a pillow.

Life admin

'For every minute spent in organising, an hour is earned.'

BENJAMIN FRANKLIN

I just love life admin! Not. Obviously. Was life always so hectic? Can I have more life and less admin please? It's a particular downer because it's invisible work and the more we do, the more it seems there is to do! Throw kids into the mix (and several school-related WhatsApp groups, sigh ...) and life admin becomes like climbing Everest in a pair of flippers. If you're wondering what happens if you just ignore most of your life admin, thinking it will somehow sort itself out, I have the unhappy job of telling you that, no, it doesn't disappear, it mounts up. So introducing a few simple planning systems to cope with it can be life-changing as it'll take away a lot of the stress of constantly feeling on the back foot. Life admin should *improve* your life not *become* your life.

Your daily to-do list

I'd be a confused wreck without my faithful list. Writing a compart-
mentalised list each day, which specifies different deadlines, is an
essential tool for prioritising. I often write my list for the next day
before bed, as it stops all the to-dos whirling round on repeat in my
head, preventing me from relaxing. Writing a plan for the following
day makes me feel in control and helps me focus on specific goals.
It takes me about five minutes to write but saves me a lot more
time where I'd otherwise be faffing trying to remember what I need
to sort out next. So, put time in your diary every single day to make
a list, it's a discipline that will pay off.

Think of the following rules when writing your master list:

* Group together tasks that need to happen today, e.g. collect-
ing a prescription from the chemist or posting a birthday
card. I always put the four most urgent things at the top and
try to achieve those as my first port of call.

* If something urgent crops up halfway through the day, add it
to the top four priority list, replacing something else, which
can be bumped down.

* On the same list, keep ongoing tasks that are important but
less urgent, such as arranging a check-up at the vet for the
cat or booking train tickets for an upcoming trip.

* If you have a list for work, you may like to keep that
separate or add it here as a distinct area. Keep work tasks
specific ('finish page five of report') rather than general
ones ('organise conference'), as it will make ticking them off
more achievable.

* Give yourself a 'power half-hour' to put the blinkers on and
power through that list.

Remember this is your day-to-day list, for help on planning lists for bigger things like moving house or a wedding, there's lots of info in the special occasions chapter on page 104.

I won't lie, sometimes tasks get added to my list a lot faster than the existing ones get crossed out. When I do tackle something that's been on the list for what seems like months (dentist appointment, anyone?), it feels ridiculously satisfying. A bit like getting up early to take on a bit of housework, I try to select the least fun to-do chore from my list as early in the day as I can. If I can cross this off, continuing to be productive feels a bit more manageable.

And what about trying to avoid the to-do list altogether? Where possible, for smaller tasks, I try to act quickly. If I suddenly remember I need to confirm a meeting appointment, I don't add it to the list, I check my diary and I send a confirmation email to the person I'm meeting. If we're about to run out of loo roll, I don't bother writing it down, I go straight into my online supermarket app and add this to the basket then and there. Sometimes cutting out the middle man is so much more efficient, even if it's only saving a couple of minutes at a time. Those minutes add up – imagine having an extra half hour each week to do exactly what you want (for more on this, read about self-care on page 86).

If you're finding things languishing on your list week after week, month after month … you know, the ones that never get ticked off, then maybe they're not that important after all? Can you delete them altogether and move on? (This does not apply to medical appointments, which I have a habit of putting off!)

Things To Do

M   T   W   T   F   S   S

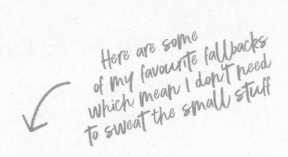

Here are some of my favourite fallbacks which mean I don't need to sweat the small stuff

Life admin hacks

SET REMINDERS ON YOUR PHONE

My phone is the hardest-working member of the Princess Planning team. It doesn't just tell me when it's someone's birthday, anniversary or gerbil's baptism, it gives me a newsflash a whole week before so that I can get a card or gift in the post. And these automatically stay in year after year. Little acts of thoughtfulness go a long way.

HAVE A STASH OF CARDS AND PRESSIES

And following up on the hack above, have a go-to stash of cards (to suit various occasions), wrapping paper and stamps around. I stockpile these whenever I see them on sale. Homemade ones by the kids are even better. You could take this one step further and have a box of generic (but lovely!) gifts for those SOS situations.

ONLINE SHOPPING

If I could spend my days meandering around the butcher's, the baker's and the candlestick maker's, I would. Failing that, buying online from one place means I don't have to schlep to the shops under pressure and probably hangry. Most supermarket apps allow you to save a 'favourites basket', so if you're really stuck for time one week, this can be a backup. My husband and I can both add things to the trolley in the sky independently on our phones, cutting even more time from our Sunday planning summit.

BUY IN BULK

If you have space to store extras, bulk-buy the essentials. You will always need household and bathroom essentials but they're easy to forget to include in the weekly shop (because, let's face it, they're a pretty boring way to spend your hard-earned cash). If you see a great deal on these, let loose, or chip in with a friend and share the spoils. Some of the following are available to buy in big containers that can be refilled: laundry detergent, washing-up liquid, soap, shampoo, shower gel, toothpaste, loo roll, kitchen paper, cleaning sponges.

DON'T GET STUCK IN A PLANNING RUT

If you've just put all your breakfast dishes in the washing machine rather than the dishwasher (with devastating consequences!) and you've left your keys in the front door for the fourth time this week, then you have too much going on. If your system isn't working, be flexible and give something else a whirl.

Visual planner

I heard about a Japanese term called *kanban*, which is a planning tool used by businesses to maximise efficiency as well as spotting any potential bottlenecks. There's now a whole host of people who've been inspired by this idea and are using it at home. It works as a visual prompt to help life flow smoothly.

On a Sunday evening, the whole family gathers round the kitchen table for five minutes and together we have a look at what's coming up for the week ahead. We take out a planner (for us it's a large printed page) and we go through the week day by day. We might see that on Monday evening my daughter is visiting a friend so she won't need dinner at home, or on Tuesday my son needs to bring a certain bit of kit to school, so he needs to have it ready to go the night before. We'll note if my husband has a meeting that means he'll be a little late home, which will give us a heads-up to prepare dinner in advance or take something out of the freezer the night before. I'll write on the planner if I need to leave for work early one morning, meaning my husband needs to do the school run. Approaching it in this way means that we're prepared and that things don't catch us on the back foot. Looking at our timetables as a family helps us problem solve and it means our Mondays to Fridays are a bit less hectic. It also ties into our weekly meal planning (see page 20) – if we know we're having a particularly busy day on Thursday, say, it means we can plan to have something quick and easy for dinner that evening, or if one of the kids has a sports activity after school one day, we'll plan to have something extra hearty for dinner as I know they'll be hungrier than usual.

Go you!

Life can be intense when you are rushing from one task to the next, and we forget to give ourselves a pat on the back if we do manage to get stuff done. Each evening, try to revisit your to-do list and put a giant tick against anything you got through that day. How satisfying is it to do that, especially if it's a job you've been putting off?

And if you haven't managed to tackle anything on the list? No biggie – accept that today wasn't cut out to be an admin day, maybe because there was too much going on or maybe you just weren't in the right frame of mind. You're not a robot, we all need time off. You win some, you lose some, or in this case:
Life admin: 0, Chaos: 1.

A word to the wise here – be wary of becoming *too* good at life admin. If you're in a couple, it's really common for one of you to take the lion's share because they are the one who is naturally better at it. Life admin can be learnt, people! Inequality will likely lead to resentment, so if you've absorbed anything from this book, it's that everyone needs to pitch in with the plan.

Self-Care

*When I nurture myself,
my inner strength thrives*

So, you've made your list, you've meal-prepped so much your freezer no longer closes and your home is clean as a whistle. You're a non-stop planning ninja, doing everything you can to hold your sh*t together, spinning plates left, right and centre! But what about *you*?

Whatever your individual situation, I'm here to tell you that a self-care plan is not only possible to fit in (no matter how full-on your life is), it is essential! I used to think I couldn't slow down because I was the vital cog holding my little world together and it would fall apart without me. But you know what ...? It didn't. It was only when I started hearing about self-care and implementing it into my own day-to-day that I realised life goes on and I was nowhere near as essential as I thought I was. It was a humbling but freeing realisation!

Modern life is busier than ever. We're multitasking like never before and the increasingly blurred lines between work and home make it harder and harder to switch off. Many of us live nowhere near extended family, meaning we don't have obvious backup, so instead of availing of help we keep on at a pace that our bodies and minds can barely keep up with. Is it any wonder that burnout is so prevalent and mental health services oversubscribed? Self-care can really help to ground you if you're suffering from exhaustion or feel overwhelmed, but it is also essential for day-to-day maintenance to prevent those conditions.

This is probably the most important chapter in the book and one I've included off the back of all the feedback I get from the Princess Planning online community.

The most common barriers to planning self-care that I'm told about are listed below – do any of these sound familiar?

✳ Lack of time.

✳ Putting others before yourself.

✳ Too tired.

✳ Bringing work home each evening (literally or psychologically).

✳ Inability to say no to demands on your time.

✳ Losing hours to screen time.

✳ Seeing self-care as a luxury to feel guilty about.

Forming good self-care rituals helps us to think positively and build good self-esteem as well as have a general recharge. It's well documented that those who have dependents (whether children or other relatives) or those who work in caring professions, such as our incredible NHS staff, or carers who look after family members, friends or neighbours, may be more likely to suffer from low self-worth, fatigue, anxiety or depression. When you are giving so much of yourself to other people or causes, sometimes we can feel drained, like there's nothing left for ourselves.

Seize the self-care day

I wish I could tell you that every day you should dedicate a big chunk of time to boosting your wellbeing, but in reality that's probably not going to be the case. And anyway, when it comes to planning self-care, little and often is the way to go, as small amounts of everyday maintenance should prevent you from burning out. There *are* opportunities in your day for micro-actions and, rest assured, I will help you find them!

Here are a few scenarios that might sound familiar to your daily routine, which on the face of it seem doomed but on closer inspection present self-care opportunities. These impromptu moments of joy can turn your day around:

✳ Your commute to the office involves your face being lodged into the sweaty armpit of a grumpy-faced man. Instead of attempting to read work emails while trying not to fall into his crotch as the train jutters along, you listen to your favourite podcast.

✳ At work, the morning completely runs away with you, so at lunchtime, even though you have a never-ending to-do list, you take thirty minutes to go outside, sit on a bench and eat your lunch.

✳ You have ten minutes before heading out on the school run so you throw your coat on and sit in the garden for a quick cuppa before pick-up.

✳ You've been asked to organise yet another fundraising event for your kids' school – you'd love to help but you're already at max capacity so you say no.

✳ There's a mountain of washing to sort in the evening but you leave it until tomorrow and run a bath instead.

Self-care is far from selfish because paying attention to and nurturing your own needs makes you *better* at helping others. Taking time for yourself makes you a better individual, partner, parent, friend or carer. It will boost patience, kindness, energy and humour, so you owe it to yourself and those around you to make self-care a part of your everyday. I no longer feel guilty about making time for myself as it makes me nicer to be around and it boosts my feelings of positivity. It also sets a good example to my kids, who now understand that Mum (and Dad!) need to take time for themselves.

If you're worried about how on earth you're going to fit self-care into your already packed schedule, see my planning tips on the following pages. Remember that timewise you will get back a lot more than you put in – for example, if I allocate five minutes of self-care in the morning, it makes me more focused and efficient throughout the day, saving a lot of time in the long run.

Positive wellbeing

Self-care isn't simply eating well, doing some exercise or remembering to go to the dentist (though those things are important!). Caring for your mental health is just as important, if not more so, because when our mental health is flourishing it tends to have a knock-on effect on our physical wellbeing. It can be anything that makes you feel like *you*. When you're juggling so many other responsibilities, such as children, our sense of self can get lost. When my kids were small, I used to ask myself, 'Will I ever wee alone again?'

It doesn't have to be a yoga retreat or £100 massage – quite the opposite. It simply means dedicating time to yourself (it could be minutes).

My favourite ways to look after myself are to:

✳ Have a bath with my best oils, a scented candle, quietly rocking out to whale music.

✳ Drink plenty of water.

✳ Go to bed a little earlier (particularly great when the bedsheets are fresh).

✳ Watch a film tucked up on the sofa with the dogs at my feet.

✳ Enjoy a piece of cake and a cuppa in a relaxed space.

✳ Paint my nails.

Other examples of self-care are:

* Going for a walk at lunchtime (particularly important for office workers).

* Saying no to an invitation if you're too busy (or simply don't want to go!).

* Reading a magazine.

* Chatting to an old friend.

* Checking in with your feelings.

* Going to an exhibition.

* Writing in a journal.

* Doing a simple breathing exercise.

* Watching your favourite TV series.

* Looking out of the window on the way to work instead of at your phone.

* Getting a good night's sleep.

Have you made time for self-care recently?

....

....

....

....

....

Write down all the things you have done to
nurture yourself over the past week.

....

....

....

....

....

....

....

....

....

....

....

....

Reset to refresh

Start viewing self-care as something integral, such as brushing your teeth or having that morning coffee. Think of it as a non-negotiable that will help boost all other areas of your life – at home, at work and socially – and therefore needs to be prioritised. The more you practise this habit, the more it'll become ingrained in your routine. If you're as planning-obsessed as I am (and let's face it, you must be because you're reading this book!) you might like to get out your weekly planner or your diary and schedule time every day for self-care. Some days it may just be five minutes and sometimes you might get much longer. This isn't necessarily about spotting a gap in your schedule – sometimes there will be no gaps! – it's about making time for essential self-preservation. This may mean you have to cancel something or ask for help to make it happen but the rewards will be worth it. Asking for backup is always a sign of strength, not weakness. But when life gets in the way – and it will! – forget about being prescriptive, just take opportunities as they come and enjoy them. This isn't meant to be yet another stressful thing on your to-do list to be ticked off.

To give you some inspiration to start working self-care into your routine, ask yourself:

What five things make me happy?

What would my dream day look like?

My Weekly Self-Care Checklist

Write a list of activities for yourself this week and tick off as you go! You don't need to do these every day!

Some ideas

Activity	M T W T F S S
Light your favourite candle.	M T W T F S S
Go for a leisurely walk.	M T W T F S S
Big bubble bath and face mask.	M T W T F S S
	M T W T F S S
	M T W T F S S
	M T W T F S S
	M T W T F S S
	M T W T F S S
	M T W T F S S
	M T W T F S S
	M T W T F S S
	M T W T F S S

Here are some things I love to slot in, depending on the time I have available. I leave Post-its around the house to remind myself to take some time out. They say things like, 'you're enough', 'slow down', 'drink water', 'you're doing great' and 'one screen at a time'!

5 MINS: Writing in my food diary or doing some simple stretches.

15 MINS: Enjoying a cup of tea on my own in the morning when the house is peaceful.

1 HOUR: Reading a book without being interrupted or catching up with a boxset.

HALF A DAY: This doesn't happen all that often, but I love a DIY pamper day, when I have a few hours to devote to myself. I run a bath with my favourite oils, light a candle and have a long soak with a face pack on. Afterwards I do my nails and put my feet up. Bliss.

Sleep for self-care

I've become obsessive about my sleep and if I don't get my seven to eight hours, I'm satanic all the next day. Catching forty winks not only makes us feel and look better, scientists are now saying that quality shut-eye is essential for memory function, healthy weight management, reducing stress and for overall lifelong good health. Hard to argue with that.

Zzzzzzzz

Turn over for my checklist for a dreamy nights rest

Night-time self care routine

✳ Keep lights down low throughout your home in the evening, using lamps rather than main overhead lights. This will help your body pick up on the signals to wind down.

✳ Ideally be screen-free for at least an hour before bedtime – our brains need to get the signal to wind down and the lights emitted by TV and phone screens confuse us into staying alert.

✳ As you're getting ready for bed, open a window and let some fresh air circulate. We sleep better in slightly colder rooms (around 16–18 degrees centigrade), so turn the central heating off or keep it on low in the evenings.

✳ Do a quick tidy, picking up any clothes or other bits and pieces lying around. It can be hard to relax in a messy bedroom.

✳ Have thick blinds or curtains to block out any artificial light, particularly if you live in an urban spot.

✳ If you are easily disturbed by noise, such as a neighbour's car alarm or dog barking, play some gentle white noise on a sound machine.

✳ Avoid caffeine, alcohol and nicotine in the evening – most of us are affected by these stimulants and they can hamper sleep. Some people are more sensitive than others, so you may find that avoiding caffeine, in particular, for around eight hours before bed is best.

Zzzzzzzzzzz

* Ban any devices from your bedroom – the temptation to scroll aimlessly online can be too much, especially if your phone is on your bedside table. Not only is the light from your screen detrimental to rest but you may find yourself getting wound up if you're reading the news or hate looking through social media. If you need an alarm clock, buy an old-school analogue one!

* A hot bath before bed can be relaxing in itself but it also gives the added benefit of raising your body temperature, and as your temperature naturally lowers again, you'll start feeling sleepy. This works for children too!

* If you are peckish before bed, try whizzing up a banana with a glass of milk using a hand blender. Both contain tryptophan, which can help you sleep soundly.

* Keep a notebook by your bed and scribble down any worries or to-dos for tomorrow that may be niggling at you, preventing you from nodding off.

* Read a few pages of a book, but nothing too heart-pumping – thrillers are banned!

* If you find that your mind continues to race around, try to help it relax by focusing instead on a part of your body, one at a time. Firstly, your right foot relaxes, then your right leg, then your left foot … keep going until you get to your head. You can quietly thank them for all the hard work they've done that day!

Our little-big world

If I've learnt one thing about starting a business and gaining a lovely online family, it's that we're all in this together. My world has opened up more than I ever imagined and reaching out to others has been a wonderful tonic – a bit of self-care in the palm of my hand.

I've had followers reach out to me on Instagram – frazzled mums mainly – feeling so overwhelmed with the pressures of life, and desperately in search of connection. I've been blown away by the openness of these people, who are so much more strong than they know! After all, isn't self-care a way to be more open to ourselves and all of life's exciting possibilities, rather than closing then down?

Know that whatever you're feeling, it's likely that someone else out there is feeling it too, and accessing support – whether that's by making an appointment with your GP or finding like-minded people online – can really help. Making this first step is sometimes the hardest part. Loneliness is a growing condition and no matter how independent we might believe ourselves to be, we all need to feel connected. Sometimes this takes a little planning, especially if we have become accustomed to staying inside our own space (physical and mental). Chatting to a dad at the school gates or someone in the park (having a dog is great for this!), making eye contact with passers-by and giving a smile can all help us feel connected. Volunteering for an hour a week or from time to time making an extra portion of dinner to drop round to your elderly neighbour – all these little–big things offer self-care for the soul.

Aim for one act of self-care a day, even if it's just a five-minute walk around the block. Everyday life is like a treadmill and if you don't deliberately press the stop button, no one else will do it for you. A rocket-fuelled pace is hard to sustain. I know that when I don't put the brakes on things get on top of me.

A spanner in the works

Life gets in the way – that's the point – and chaos prevails! You seem to fall to the bottom of the priority list after work, kids, your partner, the house, the hamster ... Maybe you've followed the advice in this chapter and tried to make time in your schedule, only it doesn't seem to actually happen because the baby's unwell, you've had to work late every night or you're so overwhelmed you don't know how to even start. Life has a habit of stopping us in our tracks and good intentions go out the window. Be kind to yourself, talk to yourself as you would a friend. What would a good pal advise if you shared your worries? It's never too late to start incorporating self-care into your schedule; start with two minutes a day and build it up from there. You deserve it!

Tick off when you've completed all your daily tasks

○ ....

○ ....

○ ....

○ ....

○ ....

○ ....

○ ....

○ ....

○ ....

○ ....

○ ....

○ ....

○ ....

○ ....

○ ....

Two

Happy Planning Special Occasions

I can. I will. End of story.

I've turned my hand to many a celebration over the years, from my children's birthday bonanzas and fundraisers at our local cricket club to my own wedding a few years back. I organised a lot of these while I was a stay-at-home mum and absolutely loved it, as it helped me to gain so much confidence when I hadn't worked for a while.

Whether it's an intimate soiree or the wedding of the century (or something in between!), I'm going to share with you all the tricks and tips I've learnt for putting together a showstopper of a day. There's also a special planning section on Christmas, as well as organising a holiday.

Now, let's get ready for a good old knees-up.

Parties

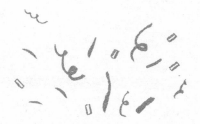

Success doesn't just happen, its planned for

I get such a buzz from seeing people enjoy themselves at a celebration I've organised. I almost get as much enjoyment in the build-up stages as I do from the party itself (is that tragic?). Whatever your party, here's my plan that will have you feeling confidently prepped and able to enjoy the event. In the words of Alan Rickman's character Harry (the scoundrel) in *Love Actually*, 'It's basic, really. Find a venue. Over-order on the drinks and bulk buy the guacamole ...' And you know what? He's not far wrong.

Let's remember our A, B, C, D, Es of planning (see page 10 for a refresher) as they really come into their own here.

It's party time

First things first, get your trusty notebook out and cover the basics. As you've gathered by now, I start most things by writing everything down. I love this part – I pour myself a glass of wine and start making rough notes about the prospective celebration. A bit of forward planning here is key, as I know it'll save me time and brainspace down the line. Getting organised also means I can party like it's 1999 when the day comes around.

Budget

This is the all-important B for budget, from our planning A–Es. Establish this from the off, even if your party is for ten five-year-olds. It means you'll stick to the plan and not be distracted by tempting extras you can't really afford (unicorn cake toppers, anyone?). It may seem like overkill to budget for a small do, but if you have several parties a year (for example, if you have a few kids), you'll find it really adds up.

Food and drinks

When planning the refreshments, think of food that suits the occasion. It sounds basic, but I've been to a summer party on a boiling day where a hearty stew was served. Weird! Consider meals or snacks that can be made in advance. If you're serving something substantial as opposed to finger foods, delicious vats of chilli or curry (weather-dependent!) or a pasta or rice salad will go down well. They can be served in bowls and people can easily eat them standing up. Going veggie means you won't have to cater for different requirements and it often keeps costs down.

* For a casual party choose foods that can be eaten without plates and cutlery, to cut down on washing up.

* Don't forget soft drinks or tasty mocktails for drivers or those who are not drinking.

* Have a punch or a batch of your signature cocktail ready in advance that people can help themselves to.

* Make plenty of ice in the week running up to the party. There's no need to buy bags of the stuff – during the week of the party, fill those trays and decant them daily into a freezer bag.

* Write your shopping list and place an order to arrive a few days before the party.

Prepare the space

If you're having your party at home, follow these guidelines to get it ship-shape:

- Clean the bathroom, putting out plenty of loo roll and clean towels. There are nosy Noras (I'm one of them) who may have a glance in the bathroom cabinet, too, so remove anything here you'd rather people didn't see.

- Clear away clutter – no one wants to see your gas bill or Tesco Clubcard out, so tidy all these bits away.

- Move items of furniture out of the way, placing them around the edges of the room.

- Think about your space – people have a habit of congregating in the kitchen at parties, so think of ways to lure them into other spaces by placing bowls of nibbles or inviting candles in strategic corners. Create a few cosy nooks for quieter convos.

- Clear space for coats, whether it's a cupboard under the stairs or a bed.

- Put up decorations or place a few vases of flowers around the house. Always cut the stems of shop-bought flowers at an angle before putting them in water, for maximum water uptake.

- If you're still standing at the end of the night, try to get one load of glasses and plates into the dishwasher and set it running overnight, so that another load can go in once you're up and at 'em the next morning.

- If needed, consider the space to ensure social distancing is possible. And provide some nice hand sanitiser.

Party Plan

OCCASION

THEME

TIME/DATE

VENUE

PARTY FOOD AND DRINK

DECORATION PLAN

CAKE

INVITE IDEAS

MUSIC AND GAMES

HELP

Party Checklist

TWO MONTHS BEFORE

◯ Select a date.

◯ Choose a venue.

◯ Decide on a theme, if you're having one.

◯ Write a guest list and send a save-the-date (via email or text is fine!).

SIX WEEKS BEFORE

◯ Invitations: whether it's beautiful written invitations through the post, an e-invite or a text, send people the what, when, where and why.

◯ Write a menu plan (even if you're serving salty snacks in a bowl), tying it into your theme, if you're having one.

◯ Write your shopping list for food, drinks and any decorations or party favours.

◯ Place an order for anything you'll need to hire, such as tables, chairs, linen, glassware, crockery, cutlery or a PA system.

ONE WEEK BEFORE

○ Write your shopping list.

○ Place a food and drink order to arrive a couple of days before the party.

○ Stock up on cleaning supplies and bin bags for the post-party tidy up.

○ Contact everyone on the guest list to remind them of the start time and address. It will give anyone who hasn't RSVPd an opportunity to do so. Ask them what song they'd like to hear at the party and add it to your playlist (see next point).

○ Create a party playlist of tunes to suit the vibe.

○ Book in some help (whether a friend or paid) for the day after the party to help tidy up.

THE DAY BEFORE

○ Warn the neighbours and agree ground rules, such as at what time the music will be turned off. Even better, invite them along and they'll be less likely to complain about noise!

○ Prepare the venue (see page 110).

Party ideas

Birthdays

A 'year/decade you were born' theme with guests dressing accordingly and some gloriously in-keeping retro snacks (cheese and pineapple hedgehog, anyone?) and themed cocktails. Try to get a printout of a couple of front pages of newspapers from the day the birthday boy/girl was born.

○————○

A party where everyone wears their least-worn piece(s) of clothing.

○————○

Characters or themes from your favourite book, for example *The Great Gatsby* or *Alice in Wonderland,* or TV shows from the era of birth (yes please to *Dynasty*-style big hair and shoulder pads).

Keep calm and carry on

I heard a great trick for managing shouty drunks who need to call it a night – tell them you have a secret to share (the inebriated *love* a secret!) and bring them to a bedroom, lying side by side so you can spill the beans. Once in situ, tell them you're quickly running to the loo and you'll be back, and with a bit of luck when you do come back, they'll be fast asleep. And if you don't fancy a drunken lump in your spare room for the night, bundle them into a taxi with a bottle of water.

Kids' parties

Try to celebrate what your child is into at the moment, whether that means having a unicorn rainbow cake or buns in the shape of Lego blocks. We always look to Pinterest and YouTube for party ideas – it's amazing the creative ideas people can dream up.

Kids love getting stuck into tasks, and if it's a party for small people, they'll need minute-by-minute entertainment, so why not combine the meal prep element of your bash with the entertainment and get those rascals working. Pizza-making parties are great because you can have a base (either homemade, shop-bought or even a sliced pitta bread) ready for each child and then a pick-'n'-mix topping bar. Simple veggie sushi rolls work well too if you have several rolling mats, or a baked potato bar and, needless to say, an ice cream station with various topping options kids can get stuck into.

If your child has a summer birthday, take the party to the local park (and save your home getting trashed!). Decorate a corner of the park with balloons and bunting, lay out your picnic and let the games commence – the following ideas work brilliantly outside and don't require any fancy equipment. It's a good idea to have an indoor back-up plan, though, in case the weather isn't on your side.

SACK RACE

An oldie but a goodie. Use a strong bin bag or
old duvet cover if you don't have a sack.

BALLOON PINATA

For a DIY pinata, fill several balloons with confetti and
little sweets. Tie a string between two points (preferably)
in the garden or, better still, use a washing line. Tie
the balloons to the string, about a foot apart, pass the
birthday boy or girl a rolling pin, blindfold them with a
scarf and let them unleash some pent-up aggression!

LEGGY LIMBO

Using some bamboo sticks and tape, set up your
limbo frame, going from easy to hard. Stick on
some tunes and a (dis)orderly queue will form!

TIN CAN SKITTLES

Stack some tins of food into a triangle, get
the kids to stand a couple of metres back and
throw a tennis ball to knock them down.

Halloween

We passed a house last year with a dry ice machine set up in the garden – its powdery smoke spreading out over a front hedge covered in cotton-wool spider webs – it was ghoulishly effective. Now imagine adding a small speaker playing a scary cackle on repeat. Shudder.

I like to open the door to trick-or-treaters with a tray of jelly snakes and spiders resting on a bed of eyeballs (the jelly kind!) and let kids help themselves. Another spooky trick is to buy a big bag of lollies, then cover each one in a single paper tissue, securing the lolly sweet underneath with an elastic band – a ready-made ghost!

HALLOWEEN BOWLING

Line up some butternut squash like skittles, then, using an orange as a ball, get bowling.

WHAT'S IN THE SPOOKY BOWL?

Fill a bag with 'creepy' objects and, without looking, let the kids guess what they are – peeled/tinned lychee or peeled grapes can be eyeballs, kiwi peel can be tarantula legs, tinned tomatoes are corpse hearts, cooked spaghetti is grave worms, cauliflower is a zombie brain.

BOBBING FOR APPLES

Fill a basin with milk and add red food colouring to create 'blood', then drop in some apples and get bobbing.

Bonfire night

We love going to see the fireworks every year in a park nearby. We pack soup in a flask and some toffee apples. If you don't have local fireworks available, pitch in with some friends to buy some and enjoy a back-garden display. Hand round blankets and cups of hot chocolate to keep everyone toasty. In terms of games, if you're hosting a party at home, the classics will fill you with nostalgia.

CUTTING FLOUR CAKE

Fill a small bowl with flour, compressing the flour as tightly as possible. With a plate at the ready, place it on top of the bowl like a lid and quickly turn it over. Then remove the bowl so that you are left with a cake mountain. Give each person a knife to take turns cutting off tiny slivers. The person who makes the cake collapse has to stick their head into the flour!

BOTTLE KNOCKING

Using an old pair of tights, tie one leg around the person's waist and in the other leg, pop in something to weight it down, like a potato or an orange. Line up an obstacle course of small pumpkins or squash, if you have them, or any other fruit and veg you have, and roll about laughing as you watch the person trying to knock them over with the 'tail' by jiggling their waist.

BOBBING FOR DOUGHNUTS

Tie some ring doughnuts onto a line of string. Using a scarf, tie the hands of your 'contestants' behind their backs, blindfold them for good measure, and following 'hot or cold' instructions from others, let them get bobbing!

Easter gathering

When the kids were small we used to have so much fun hiding little chocolate eggs around the house and garden. Even now that they're bigger, we love doing some choc-based activities in the Easter school break, such as making rocky road chunks or Rice Krispie cakes and topping them with mini eggs for the older children.

If you're having an Easter get-together with kids, here are some games they'll love:

MINI EASTER EGG STRAWS

Empty a packet of small Easter chocs onto a plate and line up an empty plate next to it. Using a straw, the child has to suck up the sweetie and transfer it to the next plate.

BUNNY HOP RELAY RACE

Your little 'bunnies' can race either by bouncing like rabbits or hopping on one foot. Make it an obstacle course if they need an extra challenge.

AN EASTER EGG-AND-SPOON RACE

Using a chocolate egg in place of a real one.

Hen do

She believed she could, so she did

If you are organising a friend's hen party, hats off to you for being a fabulous pal, entrusted with this special event. And commiserations, too, because you're in for a world of pain. Joke! Kind of …

My hen do involved thirty-six of us going to Dublin, so it was not a subtle affair! And I've got to admit, as I do find it hard to let go of the planning reins, I was pretty involved in the admin side, with the help of my maid of honour. Old habits die hard.

Hen parties are a wonderful way to send a bride off into married life with fun and positivity. Being surrounded by her best gals should give her a warm, fuzzy feeling to last all the way to the altar (or secular equivalent!). It's a lovely opportunity to spoil someone close to you, showing her how much she is treasured, and to wish her well for the future. It may offer challenges, though. People have different views about what a hen do should constitute (we've all seen *Bridesmaids*) and it may be the bride or her hens who have wildly ambitious expectations. Coupled with the fact that a hen party often comprises a multi-generational motley crew of individuals from all areas of the bride's life – school and uni friends, work buddies, relatives and soon to be in-laws. Fear not, though, a foolproof plan will see that everyone keeps their cool and a sensational do is enjoyed by all.

Think of the bride

Is she a tea-at-the-Ritz kind of lady? If so, maybe hold off on the butler in the buff. Or is she an outdoor adventurer? In which case, swap the calligraphy class for a hike. You may like to keep a few tricks up your sleeve to surprise the bride on her special day, but check in with her first to get a broad sense of what she'd like to do (and, importantly, what she doesn't). She may surprise you with her preferences.

Guest list

First things first, get this list from the bride along with all the relevant phone numbers and email addresses. This is the bride's main job and she can relax now while you get stuck in!

Decide on a date with the bride, typically around six weeks before the wedding so it's close enough to the big day to feel near but not so close that she feels frazzled. My husband's stag do was a week before the wedding – I found it stressful as I panicked he wouldn't return! Send a save-the-date email asap to give people as much notice as possible.

Be mindful of the budget

Have you ever been invited to a hen party or weekend getaway only to be told a week beforehand that you owe Michelle the bridesmaid £8 million? You had no idea it would be so expensive! Had you been told earlier you might have explained how that was a bit beyond your budget or offered some cost-cutting ideas. Remember that guests will be forking out for a wedding gift too and possibly a hotel for the actual wedding, so a hen do can be a big extra expense. To prevent any bad feeling, agree with your flock of hens a maximum budget upfront and work from there. It can be uncomfortable discussing money, particularly if there are big variances in income between people, so you may like to offer that they message you privately. The total amount should cover everything, including contingency – people won't be pleased about being charged extras when the time comes. Keep a spreadsheet and be clear about where every penny is being spent. Try to sort out money before the event so that the bride doesn't have to feel awkward seeing people scrabbling to leave a tip at the end of dinner.

Book any hotels, restaurants, transport or activities well in advance so that you won't have to resort to Plan B. For my hen do, we booked the flights to Dublin a long time ahead and flew on a budget airline, making it affordable. We shopped around for a good hotel deal, then stayed two or three to a room, so there were no complaints about the expense.

Good comms

Think of the C for communicate from our Planning A, B, C, D, Es. No one enjoys being inundated with officious emails, rolling their eyes every time they see another hen-do email in their inbox, but you don't want to be so relaxed that people wonder what's going on.

Two weeks before, email the hens or create a WhatsApp group to remind them about the:

* Venue location, date and arrival time.

* Logistics, including directions or public transport info.

* A timetable for the day/weekend.

* Instructions on what to pack if specifics are needed, such as activewear or an evening frock.

* Ask them to bring old photos of the bride to display at the venue.

Remember to keep the bride out of these emails, even if what's happening isn't a complete surprise.

Structure

If it's going to be a hen party with several activities, give people the option to pick and choose the bits they want to attend. This works particularly well for gal pals who live further away, have young children or are more budget-conscious, as well as VIPs such as the bride's mum, grandmother or aunt.

Organised fun gets a bad rap, but sitting around with a group of unfamiliar people can be awkward, so plan some time-appropriate activities (ideas coming up ahead) to keep the energy up but not so many that you're all rushing from one thing to the next.

Make it personal

Ask each hen to write the bride a letter or thoughtful note. It might include an anecdote about the first time they met, a funny story that always makes them laugh or even a little drawing. Add these letters, along with photos, to a book that you can give the bride at the end of the hen do. Create a playlist of the bride's favourite tunes to play in the background. Have a bunch of her favourite flowers on the table and her most-loved drinks and snacks.

Get those hens working on something for the wedding, too. It can be a fun activity on the hen do, which is then showcased on the wedding day, leaving all the guests admiring the hens' superb skills. Whether writing place names or table settings, making wedding favours or getting crafty with decorations such as bunting, dried flower arrangements or paper lanterns, you won't be short of things to do on your crafternoon.

Hen party checklist

FIVE TO SIX MONTHS BEFORE

○ Chat with the bride - What would she like to do and who would she like to invite? What activities would be her worst nightmare? Get an idea of the budget.

○ Pick a date – usually a few weeks before the wedding day.

○ Pick a hen party theme – you can find lots of ideas on Pinterest and Instagram.

○ Send a save-the-date email or card to everyone.

FOUR TO FIVE MONTHS BEFORE

○ Get an idea on costs, including travel and accommodation.

○ Decide on what activities will be involved.

Hen party checklist

◯   Send out an email with costs.

◯   Include an itinerary of the activities.

◯   Ask for a deposit.

TWO TO THREE MONTHS BEFORE

◯   Book accommodation, travel and activities.

◯   Send out a detailed email with the itinerary.

TWO WEEKS BEFORE

◯   Plan party bags: fill with treats, themed items, something to wear etc.

◯   Order all party items: balloons, L plates, tiara, games, and a gift for the bride. Maybe get attendees to send photos and memories of the bride.

◯   Make a shopping list of all food and drinks to take with you, plastic cups, plates etc.

ONE WEEK BEFORE

○ Double-check all reservations.

○ Send out a one-week reminder by email, including a detailed itinerary.

○ Plan some party games.

○ Make sure everyone knows the meeting time .

2-3 DAYS TO GO

○ Pack your bag – don't forget hangover remedies!

○ Get plenty of rest ready for the best hen party ever! Have fun!

Hen high jinx

Hen parties don't need to be trips abroad or country weekends away, packed to the rafters with 'essential' activities like cupcake-making classes and dance workshops. That can be wonderful if everyone has the time, money and inclination, but if not there are plenty of other more simple options, such as brunch, a walk followed by Sunday lunch, or a local night on the tiles.

Pick a theme, even if it's as simple as 'We love the bride!', think about what your friend loves and go from there. What's that? She loves nothing more than to get stuck into the roulette table in Vegas? Okay, maybe that's a bit too ambitious but could you create a DIY casino in one of the hens' homes? An inexpensive roulette wheel, a deck of cards and ingredients to make cocktails. Job done!

I set the theme for mine as Audrey Hepburn, so it was very glitz and glam. Picture thirty-five hens in little black dresses and long white gloves, draped in pearls, plus me in a white 1950s-style number. We had an amazing time in Dublin, where all the pubs played live music and we were welcomed by the friendliest people ever. The atmosphere was wonderful and we danced the night away – so while there was admin involved in booking the flights and hotel, once we got there, the city acted as an incredible host and we could all relax.

Here are some games you don't need any special kit for

WHO KNOWS THE BRIDE BEST?

In advance of the hen do, sit down with your bride and run through some personal questions. At the hen do, hand everyone a pen and paper and get quizzing. If you want to add a drinking game element, there can be a drink forfeit for wrong answers!

Ask the bride any questions you like for the quiz, including multiple choice answers, for example:

WHAT WAS GRACE SUSPENDED FROM SCHOOL FOR?

a. Smoking behind the bike shed

b. Swearing at the geography teacher

c. Playing truant

d. She was never suspended

BRIDAL TRUTH OR DARE

We played this at my hen, starting at the airport on our way to Dublin, and we were all in hysterics. My dare was to somehow obtain a pair of boxers from a random man at the airport before boarding my flight. And I managed to – a pair of Calvin Kleins no less! Ahem … don't worry, it was all above board!

LOO PAPER WEDDING DRESS

This is a really fun game, which works well at the start of a hen do when people might still be getting to know each other. Divide your hens into small teams and pass them a couple of loo rolls. Each team has to pick a 'model' to wear the dress and, once their creation is ready, the bride chooses the winner.

MR AND MRS/MR AND MR/MRS AND MRS

This is a really simple game, which will have everyone in tears – both joy and happy–sad ones! In advance of the hen do, prepare some questions for the bride's fiancé and ask them to film their responses on their phone, then send them over to you in advance of the hen party. Before playing the responses at the party, ask the hen for her answer to see how well she knows her partner. My maid of honour organised this game at my hen do and I got most of the answers wrong!

Be sure to vet the answers before playing them at the do, especially if there are any wallflowers in attendance, such as mums or grans, who may not want to hear any saucy comments ...

Questions can be anything you like, but here are some to get you started:

1   What are you most looking forward to about being married?

2   Where was your first date?

3   Who said 'I love you' first?

4   Who is the best cook?

5   Who is funnier?

6   Which actors would play you both in the movies of your lives?

7   What's his/her cutest habit?

8   Who's better looking?

9   Who does more around the house?

10   On a scale of 1 to 10, how much of a bridezilla is the bride?

Weddings

Positive mind
Positive vibes
Positive life

Dum dum de da, dum dum de daaaaa! You have found your lobster and you're putting a ring on it, congratulations. You might have met *the one* last week on the bus or come together later in life, several kids/homes/hamsters down the line – whatever your set-up, your wedding is the first day of the rest of your lives. Cheesy, but true.

I absolutely loved planning my wedding. We had a traditional church ceremony in a quaint little village in Shropshire where Nick grew up, followed by a reception in the local cricket club, which is very special to us. It was an incredible day, and while it took a lot of organisation, it was so worth it.

There isn't a one-size-fits-all when it comes to weddings, though the stereotype might conjure up images of a stately home with the bride wearing a white dress as big as the marquee outside. There are so many ways to create a superb day that will set you on your way to a wonderful life together. Tap into what you actually want and try to stand firm on external pressures. Weddings can some-times bring up tensions, especially if other family members are trying to have their two cents. If you are receiving help to pay for the wedding, the benefactors may feel entitled to dictate some of the planning. It can be really difficult to navigate this. Try to remember it's all about you and your partner and your future together.

Happy Planning

The first thing I did when I got engaged was to buy myself a wedding planner. This became my bible for the next ten months; it kept me focused, especially when it seemed like there was too much to do. Whether you're striving for an elegant, traditional affair or you're tearing up the rule book, here are my failsafe steps you can follow to make the planning process more breezy.

Show me the money

You may be a millionaire who wants a low-key shindig in your local pub or you may not be filthy rich but have your eyes set on splendour. Finances don't necessarily dictate your desires, but I would recommend having an honest look at your accounts at the start of the wedding planning journey. Perhaps you are happy to blow the budget as it's such an important, memorable day or maybe you want to rein it in so as not to begin your married life in debt. Ask yourselves these questions, as the answers will inform the steps you take. Remember that it doesn't necessarily follow that the more you spend, the better the day you will have.

When Nick and I planned our wedding, we didn't have the luxury of a never-ending budget, so we started thinking creatively about how we could get the wedding of our dreams for less. We remembered that every October our beloved cricket club hold an annual ball set up beautifully in a huge marquee. It occurred to us that maybe we could hire it out for our wedding while the marquee was up, meaning we'd benefit from all the amazing decorations already there, for no extra cost. Luckily the local church could accommodate us on this weekend so we didn't mess about getting both booked.

Word to the wise: I've heard of many a keen bride blowing the budget on the dress and then having to make compromise after compromise on important things, like the venue and catering. Of course, the bride feeling and looking fabulous on the day is essential, but you don't need to break the bank in a Vera Wang to do so! The biggest expense to concentrate on should be the wedding reception, as that's where you and your guests will spend most of the time.

Remember to add contingency to your budget, as something unexpected might crop up, and if it doesn't, you can always use it for a lovely treat on your honeymoon. We managed to come in under budget, so a couple of weeks before the wedding we booked a videographer, which was something on our 'maybe' list.

Wedding Budget Tracker

WARDROBE	ESTIMATE	ACTUAL COST
Wedding dress		
Veil/Headdress		
Shoes		
Groom's outfit		
Bridesmaids' dresses		
Accessories		
Hair and make-up		
Ushers' outfits		
CEREMONY	**ESTIMATE**	**ACTUAL COST**
Ceremony fees		
Transport		
Rings		
RECEPTION	**ESTIMATE**	**ACTUAL COST**
Venue		
Flowers		
Decorations		
Wedding favours		
Food		
Drink		
Photographer		
Cake		
Music		
STATIONERY	**ESTIMATE**	**ACTUAL COST**
Invitations		
Order of Service		
Place cards		
Menus		
Thank you cards		
Postage		
TOTAL		

Your vision

What does your dream wedding look like? Maybe you've had it all worked out since you were six or perhaps you don't know your lilac from your lilies. Creating boards on Pinterest or real-life scrapbooks can really help you home in on styles you like, especially if you're not totally sure what that is. Create a board and then start adding images that take your fancy. You may find when you revisit it that you have selected similarly styled pics and that can help you focus. Your partner can do the same and once you compare boards it will show you if you're on the same page (hooray!) or if your individual visions need some aligning. I found going to a wedding show or two really helpful, if only to give ideas for decorations that I could copy for my DIY approach.

Nick had strong views on the location for our wedding, but the aesthetic side was my baby! I had a vision straight away of the wedding that I wanted, which was a rustic country theme with a pretty pink colour scheme (I have always been a girly girl!). Pink appeared everywhere – from the bridesmaid dresses to the bridal bouquet to the groomsmen's ties. I am very hands-on and knew I would want to get involved with a bit of DIY styling.

Roll up, roll up

Putting together a guest list can be one of the more lively areas of wedding planning and often where wider family stick their oars in. Should you invite second cousin Jack and his new boyfriend Leon, even though you haven't seen Jack in years and you've never met Leon? What about Sandra from the office – you went to her do four years ago, but now you're in different teams and don't chat much. As a wise gran (the Queen) once told her grandson (Prince William), if you're getting overwhelmed when it comes to planning your wedding guest list, start by writing down your closest friends and family and work from there. Beginning with the inner circle and working outwards will mean you have your priorities covered. Have a contingency list of those 'maybe' guests who you can invite if circumstances change (such as others not being able to come or unexpected savings in the budget meaning you can invite more guests).

Ceremony and reception venue

Whether it's your favourite pub, the village hall or a beach in Bali, booking your venue and confirming the date of your nuptials is the biggest task on the list. We were keen to book somewhere that held happy memories for us, and the cricket club is where all three children, Nick and his dad have played.

Traditional venues are often booked well over a year in advance, so if that's your bag, start looking and get booking. Keep in mind that some venues will come as a package alongside catering, equipment such as a sound system and sometimes a registrar. Others, though, will require you to book everything separately, which can put a real strain on your time. That field with the tumbledown shed may be cheap as chips to hire and provide a beautiful Turner-esque backdrop, but bear in mind that you'll need to hire everything separately and costs can mount up.

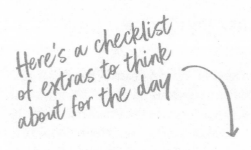

Here's a checklist of extras to think about for the day

○ Tables, chairs and table linen.

○ Crockery, cutlery and a variety of glassware.

○ Catering and bar set-up.

○ If you are supplying your own booze, check to see if your venue has a corkage charge. Many off-licences offer a sale or return deal, meaning unwanted leftovers won't be a problem.

○ Portable heating or air conditioning, depending on the time of year.

○ Wedding and public liability insurance.

○ VAT – many suppliers add 20 per cent VAT onto the bill, which can take you by surprise, so remember to ask everyone whether their quote is VAT-inclusive or exclusive.

Gather your tribe

This is the time to put together your A-team – friends who'll support you through this momentous step, be up for some planning delegation and who will forgive the occasional bridezilla moment. Don't be afraid to pull in some favours too – people will be flattered to be asked. Got a pal who's a dab hand at baking? Could they make the cake? Is there someone close to you with an artistic flair who might help with the stationery? When I was getting wed, I looked to family and friends, who provided help with cake making, photography, floristry and even an electrician to help with lighting. What a talented bunch! A friend also offered their home in Portugal for Nick's stag do. People from our cricket club venue all helped so much and it turned into a real community effort. There was no greater present than them helping with the day, saving us not just money but stress, too.

Envisage your ceremony and think of who you'd like up there with you, making it super personal. We wanted the children to be a big part of the day – Lewis and Reubin were groomsmen and Harriet was my bridesmaid. I can't tell you how special this was for us, it's a beautiful memory for them too and we often talk about the day. Reubin was only six but he gave an amazing little speech! He is definitely his mother's son – he had written it down so it was ready to reel off. He thanked everyone for attending and made a few jokes about how we wouldn't be standing by the end of the day. It was so sweet. Having these moments makes you realise that it's the people there celebrating with you that far outweigh the napkins chosen or the perfect shoes you spent ages looking for.

Logistics

We've all seen *Don't Tell the Bride*, where the typically hapless groom has booked a pretty church for the wedding and then a (probably bizarre) venue for the reception – only it's fifteen miles away and he hasn't booked any transport between the two for guests. Don't be that guy. Try to envisage the whole day, both from your perspective and that of your guests, and it'll help you anticipate any kinks that need working out.

Consider:

* Transport and parking – providing train, bus and taxi info if relevant.

* Accommodation options to suit a variety of budgets.

* Any special sartorial advice, for example, make it clear if you're having drinks on grass so that stiletto heels should be worn with caution.

Create a simple website, including the web address on any wedding correspondence, which outlines all logistical information. You don't have to be Mark Zuckerberg to make a website, there are accessible templates online that you can follow, and in the long run it'll save you time (and patience) when you are swamped with queries from your guests.

Think about the oldest and youngest members of the party – will your grandad be able to abseil down the cliff-face to watch you exchange vows during your climbing-themed wedding? Will your nine-month-old niece be able to stay awake for your moonlit ceremony on the beach? And if the point is to arrange a wedding that deliberately excludes people by being obscure, that's fine too, but be warned, it can backfire on you! My friend once organised her wedding in Morocco, as she wanted to keep it small and intimate. So as not to offend anyone she invited all her extended family, wide circle of friends and colleagues, assuming most of them would not be able to make the trip. Except they all thought Morocco a wonderful spot for a holiday and they almost all accepted. Awkward.

You might have been engaged for years, perhaps never quite getting round to actually tying the knot, or it could be a whirlwind romance where you are planning your wedding day with only a few weeks' notice. Nick proposed on my birthday in December and we got married ten months later, so the timings that follow are loose and can be adapted to your own deadline. The main point is to try to tackle as much as you can in advance, preferably at a steady pace, leaving you relaxed and prepared in the immediate run-up to the big day.

Your wedding checklist

○ Write the guest list.

○ Book the venue(s) and a registrar, if needed.

○ Send save-the-dates.

○ Book a caterer for food and drinks (if separate to the venue).

○ Hire a band or a DJ.

○ Book a photographer.

○ Book a florist.

○ Book hair and make-up stylists.

○ Choose a theme, if you're having one.

SIX TO NINE MONTHS BEFORE

○   Give legal notice to wed.

○   Shop for bridal party outfits.

○   Create a gift register, if using one.

○   Go dress (or suit!) shopping.

○   Send invitations.

○   Book honeymoon.

○   Order wedding cake.

○   Book transport, if needed.

○   Work out timings for the day.

○   Buy wedding insurance.

THREE MONTHS BEFORE

○   Contact any guests who haven't RSVPd.

○   Do the table plan.

○   Buy wedding rings.

○   Order any decorations you need to style the room and tables.

○   Choose readings and readers – if you and/or your betrothed have children, this can be a lovely opportunity to make them feel included.

○ Make any beauty appointments you need for the week running up to the wedding (see beauty checklist on page 147).

○ Buy shoes and accessories for the day.

○ Have a fitting for the dress (or whatever you're wearing).

ONE MONTH BEFORE

○ If you or your friends are having hair and make-up done, create a schedule outlining times and who needs to be where, when.

○ Catch up with the photographer and pass him or her a list of shots you want captured.

○ Delegate, delegate, delegate. This is the time to call in some favours.

TWO WEEKS BEFORE

○ Circulate a call sheet, detailing who's doing what jobs, where they need to be and at what time. Add phone numbers to the call sheet and politely ask that you not be contacted unless necessary.

○ Contact all your suppliers to confirm timings, etc.

○ Finalise any speeches or vows, if writing your own.

○ Buy any thank-you gifts for those who have helped – these can just be small tokens to show your appreciation. Have them wrapped, labelled and ready to go.

○ If you're going on honeymoon, now's the time to pack and order any essentials you need to take with you. Fill up mini bottles with any toiletries you need (and keep the empty bottles afterwards so that they can be reused on your next trip). You don't want to be packing your case the day after the wedding.

○ Have your final fitting.

○ Break in shoes.

○ Think about finding your something old, new, borrowed and blue.

ONE WEEK BEFORE

○ This week should be kept as clear as possible, with as much of the planning now complete or delegated.

○ Now's the time for a bit of self-care. Try to turn in early each evening and don't bring your phone into your bedroom.

○ If renting anything such as a suit or dress, collect these this week and have them ready to go.

Happy Planning

○ Print out spares of the ceremony readings in case readers forget theirs.

○ If staying outside your home before or after the wedding, pack your overnight bag.

○ Pack an essentials bag, too, including safety pins, boob tape, deodorant, plasters, toothbrush, lip balm and breath freshener.

This week is also when you start your bride beauty seven-day countdown checklist.

These are by no means essential, but some brides like to book:

○ Spray tan.

○ Manicure and pedicure.

○ Waxing.

○ Haircut and/or colour treatment.

○ Massage (though avoid a facial in case there's any reaction).

ONE TO TWO DAYS BEFORE

○ Drop off anything to the venue, such as decorations, flowers, table settings, wedding favours, table plan and gifts for your bridal party.

○ Entrust the wedding rings to someone (very!) reliable.

○ Depending on where you're getting ready, pop some bubbles in the fridge and have breakfast and snacks ready to go for the wedding day.

THE BIG DAY IS HERE!

Hopefully you'll wake up feeling refreshed but often that's not the case as excitement and nerves may have had you tossing and turning through the night. Don't worry, it's likely that adrenaline and endorphins will get you through the day. If you do find yourself flagging at any point, try to steal five minutes away by yourself or with your partner – go somewhere quiet and just sit with your eyes closed. This can be very restorative and give you the little boost you need to get back out there.

Eat breakfast. You might be full of nerves, but you have a long day ahead and some fuel in the tank is necessary, especially as the fizz is likely to be flowing from early on! Even if it's only a banana and a slice of toast along with a big glass of water, your belly will be grateful later.

Allow plenty of time to get beautified and make sure you are ready at least 45 minutes before call time.

Twelve Week
Wedding Countdown

Write down your weekly priorities here

WEEK 1	**WEEK 2**	**WEEK 3**
WEEK 4	**WEEK 5**	**WEEK 6**
WEEK 7	**WEEK 8**	**WEEK 9**
WEEK 10	**WEEK 11**	**WEEK 12**

Wedding self-care

Being engaged is such a special time, so it really helps to do the planning gradually so that you're not overwhelmed as you get closer to the big day. A couple of weeks before the wedding, you're going to want to start winding down. This is a time to look after yourself, getting rest and putting your feet up (apart from when you're breaking in those shoes!).

Spend quality time with your partner – what you're about to do is about your future and your marriage, not just one day of partying. Talk about what you're most looking forward to *after* the big day. Each of you write down three things that excite you most about being married and then compare notes. Focusing on what's important to you as a couple can give a bit of perspective if wedding admin is taking your sanity.

Write three things that excite you most about being married:

1 ....

....

....

2 ....

....

....

3 ....

....

....

Plan for the worst, hope for the best

If you are getting nervous about the wedding and thinking of things that might go wrong on the day, jot down your concerns. Some of these might be rational, e.g. I'm worried we'll run out of booze and there'll be a riot. The solution: increase your hooch order. Some might be out of your control, as Alanis Morissette testifies, 'It's like rain on your wedding day,' (not ironic, for the record, just annoying). In those instances, just writing them down can help you let go of the worry. Try to remember that even if things don't go exactly to plan, you can still have a brilliant day and it's unlikely anyone else will notice. Share this list with your best pal and let them figure out any issues that crop up on the day so that you can be distraction-free.

Worries to let go of:

....

....

....

....

....

....

....

....

....

....

Holidays

*Difficult roads
often lead to beautiful
destinations*

There are few things more joyful than booking a holiday and spending the months and weeks in the run-up to it getting all excited, imagining yourself there. Sometimes it's the thought of my summer getaway, especially on a cold February day, that keeps me going. I know travelling abroad can be a headache, especially with kids, but I try to be undaunted as the results can be amazing, and a bit of planning (yes, I know I'm a broken record) really does help to make it a stress-free, fun break.

Holiday budget

In the budget section (see page 36) I talked about having a special bank account to save for holidays, and this has been a brilliant motivator for my husband and I – even if you're just sticking in a few pounds a week, it all adds up. As a family, we have always thought that all-inclusive breaks worked out the better option for us as we don't want to be cooking, and you can get some great deals. Paying the bulk of costs upfront means that once we go, we only need to take a bit of pocket money.

Put your Princess Planning crown on and get researching. Like most things, booking early almost always gets you the best prices, especially when it comes to travelling abroad during the school hols. I use comparison websites to check both package deals and booking flights, accommodation and transfers separately – there's often a big variation for the exact same trip. You could consider using a travel agent – I know that seems like a bit of a blast from the past, given our ability to now book our own getaways with the click of our mouse, but they really do have invaluable expertise. I know people who have used them for longer-haul holidays, such as to Australia, where there were various internal flights and day trips to work in, and in these cases using a travel agent actually saved them money in the long run as they had so much experience of local deals.

There are other clever ways to get a much-needed getaway, even if the pennies are tight. There are lots of house-swap websites where you choose where you want to go then swap with someone who has the same idea about your place (think Kate Winslet and Cameron Diaz in *The Holiday* – then lower your expectations!). Or maybe you could rent out your home while you're away to fund your expedition. If you're renting, you'll just need to check your lease agreement first.

Choosing the right destination

When the kids were younger, we would go on sun, sea and sand holidays as it seemed much easier than exploring cities. The kids loved the freedom of playing outside and we could all relax with our buckets and spades (and maybe a cocktail or two for the grown-ups!), without the need to venture too far from the hotel.

You'll likely have a rough idea of the type of break you want, for example, if you've had a hectic few months or year, maybe avoid a city break and opt instead for a trip where you can put your feet up with your nose in a book. Or if you've been cooped up in an office, perhaps an outdoorsy adventure, like walking or skiing, is just what the doctor ordered. Similarly, if the idea of airports with their is-this-face-cream-100ml-or-less?-induced panic fills you with fear, you could pack up the car instead and go more local. Listen to what your body and mind are telling you and take it from there.

Remember to also consider:

✳ How much time you have and what's realistic, i.e. going to New Zealand for the week might be pushing it!

✳ The weather – look at annual average temperatures at your holiday destination for the week(s) you're going.

✳ If you're going with kids, look at what facilities/activities are on offer for their age group.

✳ The environment should be suitable for you/your group; for example, a top-floor apartment with no lift will likely not work for buggies or those with restricted mobility.

✳ Always read reviews of the destinations and accommodation before booking.

✳ Once you've whittled down the destination, look at travel blogs (we like scrolling through Pinterest or YouTube for them) for local tips on where to eat or to find secret must-see spots off the typical tourist trail.

Build an itinerary

It sounds really obvious but I have taken holidays where the weeks and month before the trip have been so full-on with work, parenting and life admin in general that I've barely had a chance to pack my case, let alone look in a guide book. If you've done this too, this means that on arrival you're still trying to catch your breath and it takes longer to switch off from the responsibilities back home. I've heard of friends going to the Louvre Museum in Paris and forgetting to see the *Mona Lisa*, just because they weren't able to make a little plan in advance.

I do try to fit in a little bit of online research ahead of the trip, or to gather a few tips from friends who may have been to the holiday spot before. It's really exciting to sit down with the family in the weeks preceding the trip, each of us choosing one or two things we really want to see or do, and then writing it down. My kids always love helping to build our itineraries and it's a good skill to learn – little planners in the making!

If you're going on a blissful sun-lounger-type trip or something adventurous like mountain biking, you're probably less likely to need to plan an itinerary for each day. If you're off sight-seeing, though, it will really help you get the most from your trip. I took two of my kids to Kraków, in Poland, for a last-minute October half-term escape and we had the best (surprisingly sun-filled!) few days. I had done some quick homework, making a rough plan with the kids for what we'd do each day. We had a cruise on the river, visited the salt mines and strolled around the royal castle. I knew from reading a few online reviews of the city that Uber was a super-efficient and cheap way to get around – pretty much every journey worked out as £2 and it meant we could pack a lot in. We fell in love with Poland, so the next trip on our wish list is Warsaw.

I like to make the most of trips like this, but not every second needs to be scheduled to within an inch of its life. The point is to relax, after all, so it's nice to get a bit of down time too – sometimes I have to remind myself of this as I'm naturally a go-go-go person! Some of our happiest holidays have been spent meandering around with no end destination in mind, pottering in and out of shops or stopping for a snack at a café with delicious-looking cakes piled high in the window. Bumbling about without being in a rush is one of life's great pleasures.

Helping young children cope with travelling

For kids, the journey can be just as exciting as the destination. But it can be overwhelming too. Going on public transport – whether that's a coach, train, ferry or plane – can be quite an undertaking for a small child. A big change from their daily routine, the busyness of train stations and airports, picking up on parents' stress, missed nap times and hanger can all lead to meltdowns. With a bit of forward planning, though, we can nip all these issues in the bud. In the weeks before you go, start talking to your child about some of the A–B elements of your trip, so that it's not too surprising when it comes around. If your child is taking their first long plane trip, you can prepare them at home by lining up some kitchen chairs in a row of three. They can practise walking up and down the 'aisle', saying 'excuse me' to fellow passengers and learning that the seat in front isn't a punch bag. If nothing else, they'll find it funny pretending the kitchen is an airplane! Pack them a surprise little bag of things to keep them amused, adding newly bought items such as stickers, colouring pencils, a notebook and some reading books.

Tips for packing a case

If you've ever worn five jumpers on a budget airline flight (quietly overheating so much you almost pass out) just to get out of paying for excess luggage, these tips are for you!

* Keep documents in clear folders or mesh envelopes. Take a pic of each of these items on your phone so you have a backup.

* Use packing cubes in your suitcase, which help organise your belongings and make finding things at the other end easier.

* Roll your clothes rather than folding them, as this makes them less wrinkly and also saves space.

* Wrap any delicate clothes in tissue paper.

* Plan your outfits so that you don't over-pack. Remember the joyful invention that is travel wash – a little tube or bar of soap goes a long way and allows you to wash a few staples in the sink and dry them overnight.

* Always pack a travel first-aid kit of basics like antiseptic wipes and plasters.

* Divide any medication and pop it into different bags in case any luggage gets lost on the journey.

* If you need to adhere to a weight limit, weigh your bag at home first, using bathroom scales. If the case won't stay on unaided, hop on there first and make a note of your weight, then get on there with the bag and subtract your weight. The mental arithmetic will keep the brain young. Bonus.

Handy hand luggage

Whether you'll be choppered into your destination or you're hopping on a coach, having a bag close to hand with some essentials can make travelling easier.

* Bag within the bag: okay, it sounds OTT, I know, but it drives me mad trying to dig out my keys/purse/phone from the bottom of my bag. I now keep them in a smaller bag within my handbag, so that I can grab them easily.

* My children's baby days are long over, but I find baby wipes are a travel must for any spills or smears.

* Pack some snacks to keep the energy up that can't get squashed and sticky, such as nuts, dried fruit, crackers and biscuits.

* Don't forget a spare pair of undies, socks and a t-shirt in case your luggage temporarily decides to go on a holiday of its own.

Happy Planning

All present and correct

Follow the checklist before you go. You do not want to be running around in a mad panic the night before or, dare I say it, the morning of your much-anticipated trip.

Packing checklist

WHEN BOOKING

○ Sorry to state the bloomin' obvious but if you're travelling abroad, make sure each passport is in date (and within date for the return journey too!). Time seems to fly between lining up your child for their passport picture and then finding it's expired. If you want to win a gold medal at the planning Olympics (and I know you do), set a reminder in your online calendar (even if it's years away) for four months before the expiry of every passport in your household.

○ Consider journey times, including transfers, and whether they'll be manageable for all members of the family, whether you have a baby or someone elderly travelling with you. You may decide the arduous travel is worth it for the amazing destination, but it's always best to think ahead.

○ Check if visas are necessary and work the cost into the budget.

○ Get insurance – especially if travel advice is likely to change.

ONE WEEK BEFORE

○ Get all your paperwork ready: passports, booking confirmations, visas. These things have a habit of going amiss, so gathering them all up several days before will give you extra time if they're not in the first place you look.

○ Put together an activity pack if you are travelling with younger children; buy new items, but they don't need to be expensive – things like stickers, crayons and paper are all good.

○ Plan a rough itinerary of things you want to see and do while away, and get the whole family involved.

TWO DAYS BEFORE

○ Pack, pack, pack. Be ruthless here, less tends to be more – unless you're going on an adventure holiday that requires you to bring lots of kit.

○ Let children pack their own bags: this may require a bit of supervision for younger kids to ensure they pack appropriate stuff but it's a good habit to instil.

NIGHT BEFORE

○ Have all luggage packed and ready to go, and leave it close to the front door.

○ Get rid of anything in the fridge that will go off while you're away.

○ Have something in the freezer that can be easily cooked on your return – and can be heated up from frozen. I always keep milk in the freezer, too, which I leave to defrost the evening we arrive home, meaning there isn't a scramble to the shops just so that I can make my much-needed morning cuppa.

○ If you're worried about security, set lamps on timers to come on while you're away (double-check any safety instructions for these).

○ If you're leaving early in the morning, have some portable breakfast ready to go in containers that can be discarded afterwards (such as yoghurt pots) – overnight oats work well.

○ Have a quick wipe-down of kitchen and bathroom surfaces – it's always nice to come back to a clean home.

○ Have your travel documents ready (whether a printout or saved e-docs in a folder on your phone) in the order you need them, e.g. coach tickets to the airport, flight check-in, hotel confirmation.

○ If using public transport, build contingency time into your travel to the airport, train station, etc. Feeling anxious about missing your connection because your bus has broken down is a buzz kill.

Happy hols

If you are as partial to writing things down as I am, keep a little holiday journal of all the lovely things you did (or didn't!) do. You can jot down any thoughts or intentions for your return – sometimes having a little break from the routine can fill us with energy.

Reset on stress

Have you had a blazing row with your partner about how to correctly fold the buggy? Shouted at your teenager for whingeing about being bored? Travelling is stressful and doesn't always bring out the best in us. On top of that, there's the expectation that it's going to be The. Best. Holiday. Ever. Which is a lot of pressure. You may have scrimped and saved to get here, made sacrifices that your kids will never know, and all of that can build up inside you for a pressure-cooker moment. It's never too late to call an argument amnesty and have a reset. Try to remember all the reasons why you wanted to get away in the first place. Breathe in for four counts, out for six and imagine your body filling with calm.

School Holidays

Be a flamingo in a flock of pigeons

Six weeks off school in the summer, along with various one- and two-week hiatuses throughout the year. Happy children and contented parents frolicking through meadows, having a wonderful break from the routine. Bliss, right? Or perhaps your kids' holidays cue frazzled phone calls the week before the break begins, trying to get them onto sports/arts/drama camps, only to be told they're all booked up. Argh! Whether you are a stay-at-home parent, work for a company and therefore have limited annual leave, work for yourself meaning the show must on or have no backup in terms of a partner or wider family, you will likely have felt the struggle. School holidays should in theory be a time of rejuvenation, spending quality time with our children without the stress of getting out of the door by 8 a.m., washing sports kits and haranguing them about homework. But the holidays come around so quickly and it can be pretty daunting keeping the kids entertained (and out of trouble!) for such a long time.

During the school breaks, it's all hands to the pump in our house, and a bit of a juggling act between Nick and myself, alongside help from grandparents. The reality of running a business *and* being a mum means the work doesn't stop just because school has. It is handy, though, that I can usually take time off during the day, then get back to work packing up orders in the evenings. We try to go away during the summer for a week, often around week four or five of the holidays, so we have something to look forward to. Flights can be so expensive at this time of year, so we usually stay in the UK and explore the local areas along the coast in the south west. We spend hours exploring coves, finding new villages, crabbing and playing beach cricket – it's heaven for the kids (and the dogs!).

*Here are my top tips
to help you plan for
the school hols:*

○ If you need to take annual leave, book it in as far in advance as possible.

○ Talk to the kids about what they'd like to do and discuss options together.

○ For the shorter holidays, plan a structure for each day, ideally a mixture between action and downtime.

○ Create a shared calendar with other parents if you are combining childcare.

○ Get the planner out the week before the break and fill in what's happening each day so that both you and the kids know what's going on.

○ Stock up on healthy snacks! Hungry kids can quickly become hangry.

Routine v freedom

Having a reprieve from the busyness of the daily grind is one of the great joys of the school hols. Enjoy this bit of space as well as cramming stuff in. I've found that it can work well if a busier day, say if there's been an outing, is followed by a more relaxed day, closer to home.

Don't feel pressure to always be doing things. Boredom actually fosters their imagination, helping them to find things to do for themselves.

I like to ease up on the schedule while not ditching the routine completely. We have always encouraged bedtime at the normal time during the holidays so that they're refreshed for the next day and don't become cranky and over-tired. Keep a structure, setting limits on technology like iPads and consoles – a routine gives shape to the day and reduces any power struggles.

Fun ideas for kids

CRAFT

We have a rainy day cupboard at home dedicated to arts and crafts. It's full of bits and pieces I've collected over the years – paints, pencils, paper, glitter glue, feathers, sequins – often sourced for next to nothing.

EXPLORE

Museums, galleries, libraries and local parks often have free events on during the hols.

DISCOVER

Smaller kids love a chance to roam – go to the park with a list of things to gather along with a bag to collect them in. Search for fallen leaves, pebbles, feathers, pine cones, conkers and small sticks, depending on the season, ticking them off the list as you find them.

LIMIT SCREEN TIME

This is especially important during the day as it can lead to kids being lethargic and cranky.

BAKE

Get messy in the kitchen and enjoy the goodies when they come out of the oven. Kids find eating their creations so satisfying – it's really sweet to see them so proud.

EXERCISE

Simple activities, like making dens, going on bike or scooter rides, visiting skate parks, making obstacle courses, having picnics and playing ball games help expend lots of energy.

IF IN DOUBT, GO OUT!

Get outdoors when you can – remember, there's no such thing as bad weather, only bad clothing. Spend time in the garden, if you have one, planting some bulbs or flowers, or go to the park or the woods to search for bugs.

If you've exhausted everything on the list and they are still bored, ask the kids what they want to do. Mine have come up with some cracking ideas that I'd never have thought of.

Embrace the collective

I've found that over the school holidays there really is strength in numbers. We have often taken our teens' friends with us on day trips and short breaks and then our kids have gone off with their friends' families. It keeps the children entertained and gives parents a bit of a break.

Have you got any special skills? Doing a child 'swap' with friends during the holidays, for an afternoon or morning, is easier than it sounds. For example, if there are five sets of parents, when 'borrowing' each other's children for a half or even full day you can create a sort of informal 'camp' and lighten the load for you all. And by skills, don't worry, I don't mean you need to be a qualified surf instructor, but doing things like simple arts and crafts, cooking, coding and that kind of thing, or taking the kids on trips to museums, galleries, libraries or the cinema. The trick is to have a good structure to these days, planning in advance a timetable rather than winging it. Having a shared calendar that all parents can access is essential for logistics.

Entertaining tweens and teens

Not all our school holidays are Instagram-worthy trips abroad and, of course, like all kids, mine have complained that they're bored and their friends are all doing much more fun stuff! It's both easier and trickier as they get older, especially when they're at the in-between age of wanting to do their own thing but not being quite old enough to have free rein. I look for the most cost-effective activities locally as it's not all about spending a fortune on theme parks.

We are a cricketing family so we can spend hours together playing, and football is a firm favourite, too, so during the school holidays there are always special activities set up at local clubs. If you're booking these, put a reminder in your calendar at the start of term to do this straight away for the upcoming break. It's amazing how quickly these can book up.

I've found having some structure definitely helps them to enjoy their time off as well as making it easier to get back into school life when the time comes. We sit down with the kids before they break up and make a weekly plan together so they know what's happening each day and they can pencil in things they want to do too. It's a nice way to encourage some independence, with the kids taking a bit of ownership over their schedules.

Our kids love any opportunity to earn pocket money by doing jobs (they don't do anything for nothing!), which they then use for treats such as going out with friends to the cinema or for a pizza. We often decide together on a 'project' to work through over the break, such as a big bedroom clearout – they can earn a bit of cash, get rid of anything they've outgrown and it keeps them occupied – so a three-for-the-price-of-one activity!

During the break we put together our weekly meal plan as usual (see page 20). My gang love to eat and get stuck in in the kitchen, so we add a couple of meals during school-free time that they cook for the family. It means they can have the time to get creative in the kitchen while I can enjoy a cuppa.

I set my two teenagers up with a gym membership and it helped to keep them occupied, expended excess energy and was great for their health too. They could meet their friends there, have a swim or use the equipment, coming home tired but happy.

What if you need to work?

For many of us, we don't get to put the brakes on when the school holidays come around. You might feel relieved you're not traipsing round with the kids as they enjoy some free time or you might be sad to miss the action. Either way, there are things you can do. If you can't take time off, can you request flexible hours, perhaps to go in late a couple of mornings or leave early? This could enable you to have a special breakfast with the kids before work or to get home earlier than usual so you can do an activity together like a bike ride or park walk. If it's not possible to take any time off, don't despair, hopefully you can have lovely evenings together, finding out about everything they've been up to, or have a special movie night in.

Happy Planning

Preparing for the return of school

If we've been away on a trip, particularly over summer, I always try to come back at least a week before term begins as I really hate having to hit the ground running. Have you seen the queue outside the school uniform shop the day before term begins? Standing there for ages longer than necessary with a ratty child who wants to be out enjoying the late summer sun before the drudgery of the new school year begins is not a fun way to end the holidays. Do your future self a favour and get to that shop as early in the summer as you can.

I sometimes keep a little treat up my sleeve for the last day or two of the holidays, so that we can go out on a high. It doesn't have to be expensive, something like a family barbecue if the weather's good or a trip out for ice cream or hot chocolate. It's a nice moment to reflect on what the kids have been up to and to think ahead to the next term.

Take time for yourself, too – it can be hard occupying kids and/or coordinating childcare for weeks over the holidays. Exhausted parents and children are not the best combination. Remember that you deserve a rest as much as they do!

Christmas

An hour of planning can save ten hours of doing

Ah, Christmas … the most wonderful time of the year to some. To others, it's an over-the-top stress fest. The planning aspect is something that can initiate panic even in the most organised of people. The pressure to have a perfect social Chrimbo with a pile of gifts under a glistening tree can be exhausting. Similarly, managing expectations from children and other family members without seeming like a killjoy is quite the balancing act.

Believe it or not, there are some people who plan for Christmas all year round, doing a little bit each month – from buying discounted decorations in January, booking travel tickets in April to making a Christmas pudding in July. If this is your system and it works for you, I doff my cap. It's a great way of spreading the cost and admin. I like to get ahead too (in case you hadn't yet noticed!) but I'm not quite in that category. I work to a six-week Christmas countdown, meaning I start in mid-November. I find that it stops me getting overwhelmed as I do manageable planning, which fits in with work (which really ramps up at this time of year) and family life. I'm not starting so far ahead that I begin resenting it as December arrives nor am I on the backfoot with festive fear by starting later than mid-November. Some of the advice here is based on hosting, so skip over that if you have other plans.

So here's my gold, sparkly gift to you … my planning guide for a very merry (stress-free) season.

Christmas checklist

- ◯ Christmas jumpers.
- ◯ Take family photo .
- ◯ Advent calendars.
- ◯ Wreath for the door.
- ◯ Put up the Christmas lights.
- ◯ Letter to Santa.
- ◯ Pick a Christmas tree.

- ◯ Plan a Christmas Day menu.
- ◯ Post Christmas cards and presents.
- ◯ Visit Santa Claus.
- ◯ Watch Christmas movies.
- ◯ Wrap all your presents.
- ◯ Give to charity.

25 days to Christmas movie checklist

○ Elf

○ The Polar Express

○ The Santa Clause

○ Arthur Christmas

○ Mickey's Christmas Carol

○ Home Alone

○ The Grinch

○ Jingle All the Way

○ It's a Wonderful Life

○ The Holiday

○ Miracle on 34th Street

○ Love Actually

○ While You Were Sleeping

○ Jack Frost

○ The Snowman

○ National Lampoon's Christmas Vacation

○ How the Grinch Stole Christmas

○ Christmas with the Kranks

○ Nativity

○ Bad Santa

○ Scrooged

○ Deck the Halls

○ Home Alone 2

○ Mickey's Once Upon a Christmas

○ Meet Me in St. Louis

Festive fun or bah humbug planner

I definitely fall into the crazy for Christmas camp – I'm as perky as an elf at this time of year. Princess Planning is always super busy in the run-up to Christmas and just after because this is when we get out a lot of the orders, so it means I have to be really prepared on the home front.

At the end of November, I like to create a December planner. I get the family around the table – pretty much like our typical Sunday planning session but a cranked-up version. We get everything in the diary, including the school nativity play and end of term dates, and any parties or play dates the kids have. We also add in any festive fun we want to schedule, such as the local switching on of the Christmas lights or cosy activities to do together at home, like decorating the tree. It can be such a busy time, it's nice to pencil in some downtime too, to watch festive films or do some baking. Seeing your collective diary on paper will allow you to spot any double-bookings, logistical problems or highlight which events you might like to skip.

Don't be afraid to try something new. Traditions are wonderful and I love the cosy familiarity of these each year, but it can also be fun to adopt new ones or simply to try a few new things. Bored with turkey? Try a beef Wellington. Not feeling up for the carol service this year? Go ice skating! You can always revert next year, but you never know, you might discover a brand-new, much-loved tradition.

Budget

Budget is always at the forefront of my mind when I plan for Christmas. In November, I start compiling a list of names with corresponding gift ideas. This will make the task seem less daunting when the time comes and also gives you a good idea of the budget. My mum and dad, for example, used to save £10 a week all year round, putting it in a tin so that at Christmas they had £520, which was always a massive help.

From early October, at every weekly grocery shop we add one Christmas 'treat' item to the trolley (this could be a bottle of wine, chocolates, Christmas crackers, etc.), and we put it away in a special cupboard that can't be opened until Christmas. This way the costs are spread out and the stashed-away goodies feel like a real treat when the time comes. We now do the same thing with our children, putting aside a small amount of money each month year-round to help towards Christmas gifts.

It can be hard when children compare gifts with their friends, as well as seeing them on social media, but I am not willing to go into debt for Christmas. I know that if it was lavish one year that would be expected every year, so I try to be consistent. I always like to remind myself that an extravagant Christmas isn't worth it if it means starting the new year in a mountain of debt, so I try to be fairly strict in sticking to the budget and focus on the fact that nothing is more important than spending time with friends and family.

Gifts

Like I said on the previous page, this is an easy, must-do exercise. Write down the name of everyone you're buying for (and I mean everyone, even small gifts such as those for your kids' teachers) along with the budget for each person. Note down the gifts you're planning to buy (your kids may have given a wish list, which will help here).

I ask my children to choose something they really would like rather than any old thing just for the sake of it. I have tried hard to teach my children to be grateful for what they receive.

There are other ways of going down the gift route:

✳ Giving an experience rather than a 'thing'. This could be seeing a show, going to a sports match or even having a day of self-care, which can cost nothing (see page 86).

✳ Offer friends and family a babysitting 'voucher' so they can enjoy an evening out and you can curl up on their sofa while their kids (hopefully!) sleep.

✳ Charity gifts, such as donating to a food bank or giving an extra gift to a children's hospital.

✳ Do a secret Santa (and set a cost guide) if you feel the presents or expectations are getting out of control.

Keep track of who gave what gifts so that you know who you or the kids need to thank. Try to remember that spending time with family and friends far surpasses the number of gifts under the tree. Your kids may not remember every gift they received, but the experience of enjoying a relaxed time together will be implanted on them for life.

Christmas food

If you love cooking and can nail a Sunday roast, you're laughing, as this can be a great opportunity to show off in the kitchen. If, like me, you're not about to win *MasterChef* anytime soon, the prospect of serving up the most anticipated meal of the year to eagerly awaiting diners might be daunting! I wouldn't say I'm a natural host, so for me it's all in the preparation.

Nick and I write a menu plan for Christmas Eve dinner (usually something simple and easy to rustle up) and Christmas Day. On Boxing Day, like most people, we tuck into leftovers and I make sure I've ordered plenty of bread to make turkey sandwiches on repeat. The brilliant thing about Christmas food is that almost all of it can be made in advance, leaving the day itself more about actual cooking than prep. On Christmas Eve, you can peel carrots, prepare sprouts, parboil potatoes ready to be roasted, make stuffing, decant condiments, wrap sausages in bacon and so on, which will massively reduce your workload on the big day.

Keep things simple and don't go too nuts on quantities – chances are half the family have been on the Quality Street since breakfast and won't eat as much as you might imagine. Lay out all the food on the table so that once you sit down, you stay sitting, getting stuck into your delicious feast. It's not relaxing for guests to see the host running about dappily trying to find serving spoons. They'll be hovering uncomfortably giving empty offers of help when really all they want to do is to dig into the amazing spread. And you've earned your sit-down!

In our house, Nick looks after all the cooking on Christmas Day, starting with a breakfast of smoked salmon, scrambled egg, granary toast, buck's fizz and plenty of coffee, while we open presents. We have a traditional lunch of turkey, pigs in blankets, cauliflower cheese, carrots and greens, with lots of cranberry sauce. While lunch is cooking we play board games with the kids, which can get pretty competitive (and it doesn't always end well!). We have a buffet supper in the evening when the leftovers are laid out, we have a few drinks and watch the Christmas blockbuster curled up on the sofa.

I am here to tell you, food is not the most important thing about Christmas Day. I know, I know, you're shocked. But there's no point in slaving away in a frazzled fury at the expense of your enjoyment. A relaxed and happy Christmas is even more enjoyable than the perfect crispy roast potato.

Enjoying Christmas without overdoing it

As a dedicated meal planner and food diarist, I know it can be hard to stay on track during the holidays, especially if you are dieting.

It's such a tempting time of year, but here's my advice for not veering too far off course:

* Continue the habit of writing your daily food diary – seeing what you're eating in black and white will help you feel in control.

* Get support. As well as my family and friends, I'm lucky to have support through my social media, sharing ideas and meal plans through the Christmas period.

* Planning my meals in advance is particularly important at Christmas when life can get really hectic. We rely on the slow cooker a lot all through winter – it guarantees a hearty, nutritious meal with minimal effort. After dinner I make up some overnight oats – having it ready for breakfast when I wake up means I'm way less tempted to skip breakfast only to succumb to a pastry at 11 a.m.

* I treat myself to a dress earlier in the year that I would like to wear over the Christmas period. This gives me the motivation to stay on track so I can feel great wearing it over the holidays.

* Instead of a chocolate advent calendar, I buy myself a wax melt calendar. Limiting temptation is the name of the game.

✱ I try to stay relatively active over the Christmas period as it's so easy to lay on the sofa for hours at a time scoffing chocs. Having dogs and kids helps get me out and about and then when I do sit down in front of the telly, it feels like I've earned it.

✱ I always remind myself that Christmas is a time for celebrating so it's okay to relax the routine and enjoy myself. I've maintained a healthy weight for the past two years and indulging on special occasions has never affected it in the long term. I'd never want to put my life on hold by being too strict with myself.

My six-week Christmas countdown

Here's my trusty plan in the run-up to Christmas. If you are tweaking this for your own situation, remember to keep it or take a pic so that you can follow it each year, making it your annual go-to guide. And don't forget your A, B, C, D, Es (see page 10) – particularly D (delegation!). Christmas should be a communal effort, with everyone pitching in to help.

Christmas countdown checklist

SIX WEEKS BEFORE

○ By now you should have decided where you'll be this Christmas, whether it's hosting, visiting family or jetting off somewhere exotic.

○ Create your budget (see page 178) and stick to it.

○ Write your gift list (see page 179).

○ Book your tickets to any activities, such as visiting Father Christmas (I'm always surprised at how quickly these get booked up).

FIVE WEEKS BEFORE

◯ Get gift shopping: follow your list and get the bulk bought or ordered this week.

◯ Do a stocktake of leftover wrapping paper, Christmas cards, stamps and tags and buy more if you need them.

◯ Get out your monthly planner and gather round it with your family, adding in any engagements or appointments, as well as key dates such as when term finishes. There's usually a lot going on in December so having it all mapped out will prevent any diary fails.

◯ If baking is your bag, the traditional Stir-up Sunday is the last Sunday before Advent and it makes a lovely start to the festive season. If you're making traditional fare such as Christmas cake, think about doubling up because, believe it or not, if stored correctly Christmas cakes can last for years! Christmassy treats also make gorgeous homemade gifts and if you have kids, they'll likely love to help. Gingerbread men, candied oranges and biscotti will go down a treat and are pretty simple to whip up. You can also get ahead this way and fill the freezer with homemade delights for Christmas and Boxing Days.

FOUR WEEKS BEFORE

○ If sending cards or gifts abroad, do it this week.

○ Write your Christmas cards and ask the kids to help if they can. Writing a few a day can be an easy way to get through them, or set aside one evening this week, pour yourself a glass of something tasty, stick on some Christmas tunes and tackle them all head-on.

○ If buying a turkey and any other trimmings from the butcher, place your order now.

○ If guests are staying, do a bit of a towel and bed linen audit in case you need to upgrade those scratchy sheets you bought in 1988.

○ Write your menu plan for 24 and 25 December and a corresponding shopping list.

THREE WEEKS BEFORE

○ Do your final bits of gift shopping and get in a few one-size-fits-all gifts, such as wine or chocs, for anyone you might have forgotten.

○ Do your big grocery shop or online order, based on your shopping list made last week. Ensure you have more mundane items such as kitchen roll, batteries (for kids' new toys), bin bags, cling film and tin foil – we go through these like nobody's business.

○ Put up the tree, door wreath and decorate the house. Always check your Christmas lights are working *before* going through the hassle of putting them up just in case they're not working!

○ Buy Christmassy plants, such as a poinsettia or hyacinth, to place around the house.

TWO WEEKS BEFORE

○ Buy any remaining gifts.

○ Wrap all the presents.

○ Give the house a good going over, particularly if you're having guests.

○ If catering for the masses, check you have enough chairs, crockery, glasses and cutlery. If not, you may have a neighbour who'll be away over the break who won't mind lending to you.

CHRISTMAS WEEK

○ If you are having guests, make up their sleeping space.

○ Delegate jobs for the coming days, such as Christmas Day veg duty or making up the camp bed.

○ Think about any games or activities you might like to play on Christmas Day. It could be having Twister at the ready or downloading a quiz.

CHRISTMAS EVE

◯ You and your merry helpers can stick on the Christmas playlist and get started on the food prep (see page 180). Write a simple timeline for when food should go into the oven, using the weight of the turkey and its required cooking time to determine it.

◯ Get out your roasting tins and serving platters so that you're not crashing about searching for them tomorrow.

◯ Tell family and any visitors a rough schedule for the day so they know what to expect and when meals will be served. We always have a lovely dog walk before lunch, leaving the turkey in the oven, which builds the appetite.

◯ Before going to bed (and leaving out some snacks for Santa!), we lay the table for a special festive brekkie.

◯ Pour yourself a large glass of something chilled and fizzy. You are a planning sensation, so put your feet up immediately and bask in the glow of your incredible organisational prowess!

CHRISTMAS DAY

HAVE FUN! You've earned it.

The joy of sales

Hands up if you're one of those people who can't resist a January sale, where the lure of heavily discounted Christmas cards, wrapping paper and decorations is too much to ignore? Or is it just me? If you aren't suffering too severely from festive fatigue, it can be a fabulous way to save for the following year (and your Princess Planning credentials will be off the scale). Christmas crackers, lights and tableware often present the biggest bargains, so if you have storage space and you're not totally skint, stock up.

That's a wrap!

And quick as you know it, the festivities are over. You've no idea what day of the week it is, the place looks like it's been ransacked. The fridge is empty, the cupboards bare and your bank balance is a sad state of affairs. It can be a nice time to reflect on what went well and make a note of it for next year – whether that was something on the Christmas Day menu that went down a storm or a game that brought the house down. The celebrations are over for another year, which means the decorations come down and I always feel a bit sad on this day. I like to see it as a nice opportunity for a decent clean and purge of clutter – an opportunity to start the new year afresh.

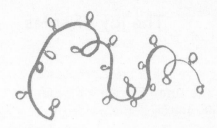

Storing decorations

✳ If your lights don't come with their own special box, wrapping them around a square of cardboard will help keep them protected and easy to unravel next year.

✳ Label containers with what's in there to make them easy to find next December or use clear plastic containers so you can see what's in them.

✳ Store smaller decorations in jars or paper cups to keep them safe.

✳ Egg boxes are a great way to store small, delicate baubles.

✳ If you're storing decorations anywhere that there is moisture, such as an attic or shed, keep them in plastic boxes to prevent them getting damp.

Three

Happy Planning Big Changes

Mistakes are my stepping stones towards success

So far we've covered how to plan for everyday life and those special occasions that make us want to jump for joy in celebration with the ones we love.

But what about when life throws us bigger changes? We may have orchestrated these, working hard to get that promotion or making huge sacrifices to save for a deposit on a home. Or maybe they've come as a bit of a surprise and weren't part of the original plan. Either way, you'll be entering a time of adjustment and having a plan up your sleeve can really help you thrive when life feels a bit uncertain.

Moving house

Always take the positives from each day, even if some days they are harder to find

W e've all heard the saying that the three most stressful things in life are death, divorce and ... moving house, and I reckon there's some truth to that. Whether renting or buying, leaving home for the first time, upsizing or downsizing, it can be such a palaver.

I have moved seven times since upping sticks from my parents' home at the age of twenty and buying my first home. We last moved when I was seven months pregnant – yes, we were just like those dippy couples on *Location, Location, Location* who think they don't have enough going on just before giving birth, so why not throw another challenge into the mix? Although, the upshot of being heavily pregnant meant that I couldn't lug boxes about, so move day was a pretty chilled one for me as I sat back and watched others do the hard work!

Let's face it, no one enjoys packing and unpacking and the general upheaval that goes with a move, but with a bit of forward planning, it can be made fun. Okay, not fun, obviously. But, you know, less painful. Get those overalls on and the bubble wrap at the ready and let me show you how it's done.

Here's a timeline to get you into gear so that you'll put your best foot forward come move day

Before the move

ONE MONTH BEFORE

✳ If you have the budget to hire movers, it'll save you a lot of energy on the day, leaving you more ready to tackle the unpacking at the other end. If considering a moving company, start gathering quotes – at least three – and when comparing them, remember to check if VAT is included as this can make a big difference. If you have any particularly valuable furniture or specialist pieces, such as a piano, check to see that they have the experience to accommodate them. Read the fine print of the agreement carefully to check who is liable for what, and make sure they are insured for any damages. Check online reviews to ensure their reliability and, if possible, ask the company if you can speak with a customer who has recently used them, so that you can get some precise feedback over the phone or via email.

* This is the time to do a ruthless declutter so that you can start afresh in your new home, with only the belongings you need. It'll make packing less arduous too. There's nothing more pointless than carefully packing something up only to get rid of it at the other end. Give each member of the family three boxes: one to put anything in that can be sold, another for charity and the third for stuff to chuck in the bin or be recycled. Some charities are happy to collect larger items of furniture without charge.

* A home is always easier to clean, make repairs to or decorate when it's empty. If the property you're moving to is already empty, sometimes estate agents, whether you're renting or buying, can negotiate access for cleaning, maintenance and decorating before you officially move. Explore if this might be possible in your circumstances.

TWO TO THREE WEEKS BEFORE

* Whether you're buying or renting, before leaving your current home, remember to contact service providers to arrange for phone lines, internet and utilities to be shut off.

* Set up a post redirection service. This is important not only so that you receive your mail but so that you do not worry about your private information getting into the wrong hands, risking identify theft.

* If you are hiring a self-drive van, book it now.

* Order your packing materials (checklist coming up).

* Organise parking permits, if needed, for both your current home and the new one, so that the delivery van can park close by.

* Book in some muscle in the form of strong and enthusiastic friends! Get help – more hands make light work. I have always had family members to help me as I know I couldn't possibly do everything myself and I make sure that I reciprocate in turn.

* Unless your kids are a bit older (and are happy to carry some boxes!), arrange for them to go to a friend's on moving day.

* If you have a pet, you might consider them having a sleepover elsewhere as some cats and dogs can get a bit put out by all the coming and going on moving day.

* In the weeks before the move, eat as much as you can from the fridge, freezer and cupboards to avoid waste and having to pack up too many food stuffs.

THE DAY BEFORE

* Have devices such as phones and chargers charged and, once done, keep these chargers in your handbag.

* Defrost the freezer (if you're taking it with you).

* Have a bag of snacks and drinks ready to keep energy up when moving.

* Take pics of final meter readings for gas, electricity and water.

Happy Planning

✳ If you are renting, take photos of the house before you leave, showing the condition you've left it in so that there are no disputes down the line.

Box clever

I find that there's a sweet spot with packing – if you start too early, you end up tripping over boxes for weeks, unable to find anything you need and losing your mind on a daily basis when you can't find that piece of paperwork or the kids' school shoes. You may also start off in a blaze of enthusiasm only to get dejected halfway through, leaving your home in total chaos. But leave it too late and you'll panic-pack – you'll feel super-stressed, there'll be no time for a clearout, the boxes will be a jumble, things will get broken and it'll be Armageddon when you arrive at your new home. Of course, it depends on the size of your house – a mansion will obviously take longer than a studio flat – but for a medium three-bed I'd suggest starting two to three weeks before moving day.

Packing tips

Make sure you have plenty of boxes, scissors, masking tape, bubble wrap, tissue paper, labels, markers and bin bags.

- ✳ Use good-quality packing boxes and tape to avoid breakages. You can pick up strong boxes from supermarkets or local businesses, or pop an ad on Facebook or Freecycle.

- ✳ Don't overload the boxes as you'll need to be able to lift them!

- ✳ Make use of storage you already have, such as washing baskets and suitcases.

- ✳ Pack one room at a time and clean as you go along, which will make both tasks much more manageable.

- ✳ Label boxes with which room they came from/should go into so that it's easier to find things when you arrive at the new house.

- ✳ Pack the heaviest things first, so that they're at the bottom of the box. Line boxes with towels and bedding to secure things in transit.

- ✳ Pack valuable items, such as jewellery, passports and any other important documents, separately and keep the bag with you when you travel to your new home.

- Keep an arrival box filled with things that you'll need immediately: phone chargers, kettle, mugs, tea bags or coffee, a kitchen sponge, washing-up liquid, loo roll, hand soap, drinks including milk, snacks to keep your energy up, colouring books, balls, toys, etc. to keep the kids occupied when you first arrive.

- Pack a box or bag of easily accessible first-night provisions: bedding, towels, toiletries, medication and a change of clothes for each member of the family.

YOU'RE IN!

- Crack open the fizz and get the takeaway ordered – the first evening in your new home is a special one. The chances are you're sweaty and tired from lugging boxes around all day, but hopefully you'll be basking in the glow of your new surroundings and, if not, you'll soon be amazed at how much a bit of elbow grease and a lick of white trade emulsion paint can inexpensively transform a place.

- When it comes to unpacking, I always start with the kitchen, getting the basics set up such as the kettle, microwave and toaster. I then start tackling the children's rooms so that they can feel settled quickly. Start by making up the beds so that everyone can get enough rest, ready for cracking on the next day.

Moving admin checklist

○ For the record, take a photo of the meter readings for gas, electricity and water on arrival at your new home.

○ Have the locks changed for security and peace of mind.

○ Prioritise getting the utilities set up as well as the phone and internet provider. This can be a great opportunity to shop around for the best deals, using comparison websites.

○ Contact the council (and the one you've just left, if you're moving to a new area) – you may be eligible for a refund of council tax.

○ Register your new address with your employer, bank(s), doctor and dentist surgeries, solicitor or will provider, children's school(s), DVLA, TV licensing, subscriptions you receive through the post, supermarket delivery services.

○ Remember, not everything can be done immediately, it takes time. Breathe, allow yourself to take breaks and keep in mind realistic expectations of what can be done. Most of all, enjoy your new home!

Starting a Business

*Believe
Achieve
Succeed*

If you'd told me a couple of years back that I'd be a director of my own company, receiving nearly a thousand orders some days, I'd have laughed. All I wanted when I started Princess Planning was to get back into the world of work but still be around for the children. I was a stay-at-home mum, so I wanted to be able to take them to school and still pick them up, but earn a living too. I hoped to be busy enough to keep myself occupied from 10 a.m. to 2 p.m., and I was prepared to work evenings and weekends if I needed to. So ultimately for me, being a girlboss gives me flexibility. My world has opened up more than I could have dreamed and I've got the most brilliant customers, whose support I value more than I can say.

I had no business background whatsoever when I started Princess Planning, just my own experience of wanting to have pretty stationery to help motivate me to keep on track on my weight-loss journey. I guessed that if I wasn't finding the planners I wanted then other people weren't either. So I took matters into my own hands and started designing and printing some simple planners. I was blown away by the demand for them. Life has been a whirlwind ever since, but I wouldn't change a thing.

Taking the plunge

If you are currently deciding whether to set up your own business or become self-employed, think about what your aims are. When I was weighing it all up, I made a list of what I thought the pros and cons were, and it looked a little like this:

PROS	CONS
Being my own boss.	Having sole responsibility for the business.
Flexibility around setting my own hours.	Lack of job security.
Creating my own schedule.	No holiday, sick pay or pension provision.
A nice work environment free from conflict and office politics.	Worry that if I'm ill one week, business will grind to a halt.
Working from home (which reduces overheads).	No job security.
Taking holidays and breaks as needed.	Working round the clock.
Having family pitch in.	Getting my head around management of accounts.
Working towards something I really believe in.	Impact on health and family life due to long hours some days.
Making my own decisions.	

In the end, I trusted my gut and went for it. Of course, there have been times when I thought, Arrrrghhhh, what am I doing?! This happens when the business is particularly hectic and the juggle with family life becomes way off balance.

In the early days of PP, I worked on my own to fulfil the orders, answer customer queries about products and help people place their orders. I had to learn on my feet as in a short space of time it became apparent that it was going to be a lot more work than I had ever envisaged. From day one, I have always wanted to get the orders out fast, as being on a weight-loss journey myself I know what it feels like to want to get started. I would always slot my job around my family, so as soon as the kids had left for school in the morning, I put my work hat on. You only get out of life what you put in, and when I keep that mantra in mind I never struggle to motivate myself to work.

I'm not claiming to be Sir Richard Branson, but I've learnt so much since starting Princess Planning and I want to share with you my top business planning secrets:

1 Follow your instinct

Putting yourself out there can be scary, but I believe there's a lot of merit in valuing your intuition. You don't have to necessarily have it all worked out, with a detailed five-year plan of intricate forecasting, etc. – I know I didn't! Of course, some degree of planning is important (otherwise I wouldn't be writing a book about it!), but projections and analytics can only take you so far. Sometimes taking a leap of faith and going with your gut is the only way. If you have an idea that you can't shake, your intuition is likely telling you to go for it. When I started PP, I didn't have much of an insight into the stationery and wellbeing markets, but I knew from my own experience how encouraging it is to have pretty planners that inspire you. I thought if I have been able to change my life through using daily planners, then I need to get the word out to others. Starting my business came from a place of huge passion for helping people. It was definitely an emotional decision rather than a totally rational one.

2 Write down your goals

What has prompted you to want to start a business? Maybe you've always had an idea you want to bring to life or perhaps you've spotted a gap in the market for a product or service? Or maybe it's the by-products of launching a business that appeal, such as setting your own hours, working from home or making your own decisions. A bit like when I got my pros and cons down on paper, make a list of what you want to achieve and keep it somewhere prominent so you can revisit it and measure your progress.

3 What does your business stand for?

Whether you're a one-man or -woman band or a massive multi-national, having guiding principles can really help you stay committed to your goals – both the commercial and social ones. Thinking about what your business stands for will help you clarify your idea and make informed first steps. When I started Princess Planning around my kitchen table, it felt right to me that I should work alongside people with similar core values to myself. I wanted to benefit my local community as much as possible, meaning that any success I enjoyed would go on to support other families. With this in mind, I chose a local printer to manufacture my stationery. Yes, it costs more than having everything made in the Far East but I love the face-to-face interaction, trusting in the skill of local experts and supporting other small–medium businesses like my own. By surrounding myself with good people, I feel inspired myself.

4 Imagine your customer

Try to envisage your target customer or client (depending on the nature of work). Think of a real person – where do they live? What are their hobbies? What does their home and professional life look like? Having a 'real' individual in mind will help you get a sense of their mindset and how your product or service can fulfil their needs. Step into your customers' shoes to see how they might go about finding you and what you have to offer – you may have the best wares in town but that's not much good if no one can find you!

5 Write out a financial plan

Perhaps the biggest obstacle for taking a leap into business is financial, and that is a valid concern. It may be that for months or even years you need to keep to your day job alongside your business project to help bankroll it. That can be really exhausting and I am full of admiration for those who follow their dream, particularly when they have to make many sacrifices for it. I would recommend trying to estimate costs in advance of taking the plunge, particularly if your business idea requires you to make an initial outlay.

Plan to lose. No, that's not a typo – most businesses often make a loss for some time at the start. Try not to view this as demoralising, you are laying the groundwork for a brilliant business framework and that takes time!

6 Identify your work personality

The joy about being your own boss is that you can play to your strengths and set your own timetable. Do you thrive in the early hours of the day? If so, perhaps setting an alarm for before the rest of the household wakes is the way to go. Getting the best from yourself is integral to the success of your business. Similarly, if you are starting a business while still in other employment, it means you might be able to work in the evenings and at weekends.

Start thinking about your work space, too, and any particular requirements you'll need. Do you need to start looking at hiring an office, studio, shop or co-working space? Depending on the type of business, you may only need a laptop and a place to sit. I started Princess Planning around my kitchen table, writing out a very rough plan in a notebook.

7 Listen as much as you talk

Talk to people about your plan for a new venture and really listen to what they say. Invite their honest feedback, even though it's sometimes hard to hear. Identify areas where you need to develop or get support, asking for help or a second opinion is a sign of strength, not weakness! Is there an opportunity to have a mentor? It doesn't matter if you're 25 or 55, learning from someone who is successful in his or her field can give you a snapshot into their years of experience. They can act as a sounding board for your plans, give you their insights and offer motivation.

8 Do sweat the small stuff

Okay, this isn't the most exciting advice but being aware of the nitty gritty is super important. Before you get started, research your accounting, tax and legal requirements.

Here some things to keep in mind, but this list isn't exhaustive:

* Register with HMRC (if you are in the UK). It's your responsibility to ensure you have ticked all the boxes correctly and fines are given even for innocent mistakes, which are easy to make first time round.

* Keep money back for your tax bill by saving it in a separate account. You don't want to be caught out here.

* Understand your entitlements – a lot of business costs are tax-deductible and there are sometimes grants available to help you get started, depending on the nature of your work.

* If you are hiring staff, contact HRMC to ensure you fulfil the legal obligations this brings.

* Trademark your company's name. I had a business trying to rip off Princess Planning before I'd had a chance to trademark the name; they were photocopying my work and selling it off as their own. So act fast with this!

9 Believe in your own worth

Embrace your inner Elle Woods here and have faith in yourself. When you are a start-up with no fancy track record to fall back on, you may meet people who, rightly or wrongly, are not willing to give you the benefit of the doubt. I found this, particularly when I was looking for suppliers. I contacted printing businesses local to me who didn't want to work together as initially the order I was placing was too small. But remember, just because you're small now, it doesn't mean you'll always be. That business missed out on a massive opportunity.

I was shocked to find out that even in my world of pretty stationery, there is a cut-throat side. I've had nasty messages, fake reviews and competitors trying to bring me down. It has at times really upset me, but I try to stay positive and remember that behaving in that way only demonstrates their bad character and not mine! I find having a business mantra – a bit like the positive affirmations I've scattered throughout the book – really inspiring. It sounds a bit woo-woo, but positive thinking really can have an impact on success, in every area of life.

Here are some simple business mantras you might like to try when you are going out on your own:

Good fortune will flow my way
My challenges will bring me opportunity
Trying is success in itself
I will earn more money than I need

10 Give yourself regular appraisals

This is where the E for evaluate in our Planning A, B, C, D, Es comes in. If you've ever worked for a company you might have had annual appraisals. Your line manager might have assessed the ups and downs of the year, analysing what went well and what didn't, while setting goals for the future. You may have found these really uplifting and a chance to celebrate all your hard work. Or maybe they weren't always the most comfortable sessions, as it can be hard having an honest look at our performance, especially if things haven't always gone to plan. Even though I'm my own boss, I like to have a little self-appraisal every six months or so. I find these so helpful to focus on what's been going well and what hasn't.

I specifically look at:

* The accounts for the previous six months, compared to the six months prior.

* A problem that occurred, for example with a printing or a shipment, and how I dealt with it.

* A highlight of the six months, which is often something like getting a particularly lovely review or feedback from a customer – these are so special to me.

11 Be prepared that life may never be the same again

You'll likely work longer and harder than you thought was humanly possible. Try to be surrounded by people who'll support and encourage you, especially as there may be times when you question your sanity for having made the jump to self-employment! Life will probably be disruptive at the start and there will be sacrifices to make – hopefully short-term ones that will lead to long-term gains. Believe in yourself and keep moving forward. Give it everything you've got and go for it.

What do you want to achieve over the next year?	By when?

Business Plan

BUSINESS NAMES

VISION

PRODUCTS ELSEWHERE

WHAT MAKES ME DIFFERENT

OBJECTIVES

HOW I'LL GET THERE

MARKETING IDEAS

TARGETS AND MILESTONES

NEXT STEPS

New Job

Be brave, be bold

I had so many jobs over the years before becoming a stay-at-home mum. Some worked out better than others. I had part-time jobs from the age of twelve and my first was in the local post office, earning 50p an hour putting sticky labels on tins. I absolutely loved it. I then went on to work in the local chip shop, which was my dream job because at the end of my shift I could take home whatever I wanted. Although I had a pretty disastrous experience there when I was lighting the kebab machine – by mistake I threw the match into a paper bag lying next to the machine and the whole thing went up in flames. I never made that mistake again!

After I left school, I did a variety of jobs, like working as cabin crew for an airline, being a sales rep, a bank advisor, working for a car sales company and then as a job centre advisor. Some of these roles I loved and others I couldn't wait to get out the door at the end of a day. No matter what the job, though, I've always tried to go the extra mile. I may not be the cleverest or the most tech savvy, but I've always put the hours in and given every role my best. In life you need luck but I truly believe the harder you work, the luckier you get.

You may be spending 40 hours a week (or more!) in your job, you'll see your colleagues more than your partner, children, wider family and friends, so it's important you find a position that you enjoy. Life is too short to devote half of it to doing something you're lacklustre about. And if you're currently in a job that isn't tickling you pink, it's never too late to do something about it and make the Sunday night dread a thing of the past. It's not enough to just tolerate your job, you need to feel passionate about it.

Start 'em young

I've always encouraged my teenagers to get out there and get a job they can get stuck into at weekends and over the school holidays. At this stage it's not really about the cash (though they do love having some pocket money) but about the experience and life skills, which are so valuable. A lot of teenagers now seem to have high expectations from life and are reluctant to get a part-time job, which I think is so sad.

My older two have had paper rounds, worked in cafés and shops, and all three of them pitch in with Princess Planning. In fact, they've been a vital part of the business's success. At one really busy point, when orders were coming in left, right and centre, I set up Lewis's bedroom as a mini HQ to dispatch parcels. We worked so hard as a family and they learnt valuable lessons from this. I always tell my kids that you have to work hard to achieve your dreams and I like to think this message has sunk in. My son Lewis had always wanted to join the Royal Navy and he applied last year even though he was pretty daunted by their rigorous recruitment process. He did find it challenging, but I have always drilled it into him and his siblings that it's all about mindset – staying positive and telling yourself you can do it. Since passing out, he's now onto his second phase of training, completing tasks he never thought he was capable of. It's a lesson to all of us to ignore that nagging inner critic and instead go for our dreams.

Think of your goals

This comes back to the A of our planning rules: establishing your aim. Maybe you've been planning on being prime minister since you were five, or perhaps you're fifty and still have no idea what you want to do 'when you grow up'. Fortunately, the job for life concept is long gone and we have more career options than ever before. It can be overwhelming knowing where to start and having the confidence to go for it, so working out your goals first and going from there can help match you up to the role that will best suit you. Whether your aim is to get more experience, work flexibly to enable you to pursue other passions, improve your commute or to bring in the big bucks, knowing what your aims are is the first step.

Assess your strengths and areas for improvements

Before you start job hunting have a look at where you stand at the moment. What skills and experience do you have right now? Are they enough to get you to the next step of where you want to be? If there is a deficit, look at how you can address that with the aim of plugging any gaps before searching, to ensure you achieve the best position possible. It may be that skills can be self-taught in your spare time or perhaps there's more training you can avail yourself of in your current role.

Your personal brand

I know, it sounds a bit corporate to talk about a 'personal brand' but in this day and age, a prospective employer will be as keen to know just as much about you as your experience. Remember the C for communication in our planning A, B, C, D, Es – it's time to update your CV and any professional career sites you use. Make sure, insofar as you can, that your online presence is respectable as it's likely employers will do their research about you. So if your social media shows you up to shenanigans, take down any incriminating evidence or make your accounts private!

YOUR CV SHOULD

✳ Be no longer than two pages.

✳ Follow a reader-friendly format, with clear section headings.

✳ Contain a punchy personal statement of a few sentences, specifying what you're currently doing and any career or experience highlights.

✳ List your experience in the order of the most to least recent.

✳ Highlight any achievements or relevant training.

✳ Proofread, proofread, proofread! A single typo will be enough to put off a lot of employers.

The interview

Congratulations! Your application has obviously impressed and you have been invited to interview. Even if you're the coolest customer in town, you need to do some prep, both about the role you're applying to, and about pitching yourself.

✳ Do your homework about the organisation you're applying to – sounding informed is essential. If it's a larger company, in addition to a website they may have social media you can check and see what they've been up to lately.

✳ Decide on your outfit the day before (at the latest) and wear something smart but comfortable – you don't want to be tugging at a hem as you sit down.

✳ Get to your location at least half an hour early and have a cuppa in a nearby café. Being stressed about arriving late will not put you on your A-game.

✳ Find out as much as you can about the individual(s) interviewing you.

✳ Prepare a short verbal pitch about yourself and top-line info about your experience so far, so that when the inevitable 'tell me about yourself' question crops up, it'll roll off the tongue.

✳ Explain why you'd be an asset to them.

✳ There will likely be an opportunity at the end to ask a question, so prepare at least two in advance in case you can't think of one on the spot. Having more than one planned out means you have a fallback option if one of your prepared questions naturally gets answered earlier in the interview.

* Ask the interviewer something about their role or position – people love talking about themselves!

* Try to find out about the company's work culture and the team you would be working in, if applicable. An interview is a two-way street and you need to find out as much as possible if the role will be right for you.

You've got the job, yay!

You've only gone and got it. Go you! Once the celebrations are over, it's back to the grind I'm afraid. Planning ahead will ensure you get the best out of this new role.

Sometimes we put all our efforts into nailing the interview, then forget to think much beyond that. But considering your intentions for the job is something we all need to consider, no matter how junior or senior the position. Have a think about what this job will mean for you both now and in the future. Is it your dream position that future-proofs your career goals? Or does it have a metaphorical expiry date, where you'll get experience for a certain number of months or years before you move in? Considering what the job will do for you in the context of any wider ambition will mean you get the most out of it.

Write down your hopes and dreams for this role, including where it might lead you if you are thinking of it as a stepping stone:

The first day

If your palms are sweaty just thinking about the first day of anything new, then these tips are for you. First days always make me apprehensive – a new routine, skills to learn, brand new faces and names to remember. They can be really exciting but a bit nerve-wracking too, so I do everything possible to plan what I can, which makes me feel a bit calmer.

* If you are working in a new area, do a practice commute. Being familiar with the route will mean you feel more in control on your first day. Aim to arrive fifteen minutes early on day one.

* Prepare your first day outfit – just like the interview, you need to look smart but feel comfortable. Now isn't the time to wear those new shoes that you haven't yet broken in. Hobbling about for eight hours on your first day is not a good look!

* Get good rest the night before. Even if you have trouble drifting off, a relaxed evening at home and an early night will stand you in good stead.

* Unless you know the area well, including local cafés and shops, pack a lunch – you do not want keel over from hunger on your first afternoon.

* Even if you're a ball of nerves inside, try to be cheerful and positive – a smile goes a long way.

* If you aren't a fan of small talk (and, frankly, who is?), prepare a short introduction about yourself as you're likely to have to introduce yourself more than once. Just try to avoid it sounding too scripted.

* If nerves are getting the better of you, pop to the loo, breathe in and out and stretch your arms and legs as wide as you can, like a starfish. Sounds crazy, I know, but these 'power poses' are proven to fill an individual with confidence.

* Show initiative but be willing to listen.

First-day jitters are totally normal. It takes time to settle into a new role – often around six months – so be patient with yourself. No one will expect you to know everything straight away so neither should you.

Give it all you've got

I don't mean you need to be a slave to your job, that will only lead to burnout, but while you're at work, give it all your energy and focus. Throwing yourself into your job means you'll be in the moment, taking pride in what you do, and your attention and enthusiasm will not go unnoticed. Ask your manager about any learning opportunities such as training, shadowing or mentorship schemes – your development benefits everyone. Try to build good relationships with colleagues but stay out of office politics as the negativity will drag you down.

As in many areas of life, clear communication is key. From day one, understand your boss's expectations of you. Try to have this brief, along with goals, in writing so there is no confusion and you can both revisit these objectives over time. Ask for regular feedback on your progress and discuss ways in which this can be tracked. At the end of every single week, write down any achievements, big or small, so that when the time comes to discuss your progress, you'll have a handy fact sheet to hand proving how brilliant you are.

Work–life balance

I've already written quite a bit about the value of self-care and I think at work it's extra important. First and foremost, being in a job you enjoy is a vital step in self-care. If you hate going in each day, there's only so much a stroll around the block at lunchtime can do to soothe your soul. Your job is likely a big part of your life but it shouldn't necessarily define who you are. Setting boundaries starting from day one will help you stay happy and healthy at work, making you more productive in the long run. Try to leave work at the door when you go home – I know that's easier said than done, especially for someone with perfectionist tendencies (who, me?), so you may well need to make an effort. Remember, you are not doing yourself or your employer any favours by burning yourself out.

Here are some simple self-care ideas – try to incorporate at least one into your working day:

✳ Use your break to get some fresh air, exercise, practise a hobby or catch up with a friend.

✳ Drink plenty of water, especially if your job has you on your feet for much of the day.

✳ If your job involves sitting a lot, move out of your seat at least once an hour and walk around and have a stretch.

✳ If things are getting overwhelming, do some breathing exercises. Deep breaths in and out have been shown to calm the body and mind.

✳ Mix up the tasks you do so that you are not working on the same thing for longer than ninety minutes at a time.

New Year Resolutions

*New day, new mindset,
new focus, new intentions,
new results*

This chapter could just as easily be called 'how to plan for change', whatever the time of year. I've gone through some pretty big life changes; some I'd anticipated and worked towards and others that I was thrown into. Along with taking a leap of faith and starting Princess Planning, the biggest conscious changes I've introduced into my own life revolve around my parenting approach and the journey I went on to lose weight.

When I first had children, I became very overwhelmed and this lasted for several years. I felt that I had lost my own identity and only existed as Charlotte the Mother. I became very reclusive, without interests of my own, and instead my life revolved around my children 24/7. I now look back and realise that I'd got stuck in a rut of bad habits, which didn't benefit either me or them. It meant that as they grew into toddlers, which is a time when typically children become more independent, mine would struggle if they weren't with me all the time. It made things like the transition to nursery so hard – it was heartbreaking at times. When I was pregnant with my third child, I made the deliberate decision to parent differently. I approached it in a more relaxed way, fussing over my son less and taking a step back where before I'd have rushed in to attend to every whim. He showed a lot of independence and I know I certainly felt more at ease.

It was around this time that I decided I needed to tackle my weight. I piled on the pounds when I was pregnant with Reubin. I craved all the wrong foods but just told myself not to worry, that I should enjoy it and allow myself to be indulgent. After he was born, I started trying to make lifestyle changes. I'd follow every diet under the sun, and I'd chip away at those stubborn pounds only to regain them. It was a cycle I just couldn't seem to get out of, as my old patterns of grazing all day and over-eating at mealtimes would return. It was only when I addressed these habits that I began to see lasting results. I was making good progress when Nick proposed to me and it was having the goal of my wedding to focus on that helped me achieve my aim of losing the final few stone. This is when I began to plan my meals and write my food intake down every single day. It was only when I saw on paper what I was eating each day that I realised I had been kidding myself.

Through making mistakes I've learnt the approaches that work, what motivates me and how to stick to the plan. It's such a boost to the confidence when you set an intention and then see it through – you'll feel like a superhero who can achieve anything!

This is your year to sparkle.

Look back to look forward

Like a lot of people, I see January as an opportunity to think about the last twelve months and also to the year ahead. I write down some of the high and lows, just as snappy bullet points. I'm sometimes surprised by what comes out, things I had half-forgotten about but that were clearly still lodged in my subconscious. This isn't an exercise to beat myself up over things that could have gone better, it's a chance to look at the challenges and see how I tried to tackle them. Of course, I haven't always got it right but I've grown from every one.

So, take out a brand new notebook and:

Write down your top five hits of the previous year.

....

....

....

....

Ask yourself, what were the five experiences you'd rather forget?

....

....

....

....

Decide what your hopes are for the New Year:

....

....

....

....

....

....

....

....

....

....

....

....

....

....

....

....

....

I always think that in order to make a plan for the future, it's good to take a look at where you are right now. It can be easy to focus on the negatives or what you think is lacking, when actually there are likely to be so many positives in the here and now. Showing gratitude for the good things in life and being in the moment can really help motivate us to strive for our future goals. Write a list of five things that you have now that you're grateful for. They could be big things, such as family members or your job, or the little things in life that bring a smile to your face, like curling up to watch your favourite boxset or eating your most delicious brekkie.

A is for aim

First and foremost, remember the A of our planning toolkit. Write down your aim for change in one sentence, being as specific as possible.

Here are some common ones:

* Lose a stone.

* Quit smoking.

* Limit alcohol to weekends only.

* Get a new job.

* Start exercising more.

* Make new friends or find romance.

Be realistic

Planning on winning the EuroMillions? Good luck with that! We can all dream, but planning resolutions that you have control of is a good place to start. Empty promises on New Year's Day to give up booze for a month, never eat sugar again after the Christmas binge, watch those pennies for the whole year ... any of these sound familiar? I've made (and broken) many a New Year's resolution in the past, only ending up feeling worse about myself instead of better when I can't stick to them.

I try to look at New Year positively, as an opportunity rather than a chance to admonish myself for my actions over the past twelve months. Keeping it real is vital – for example, I am not massively into fitness but the last resolution I made was to exercise more. As much as I'd like to be someone who spends an hour at the gym five times a week, it's just not realistic for me. So instead I pledged to do a 20-minute walk with my dogs every day. This was more manageable and a change I could fit into my life, and after a couple of weeks of doing it every day, it has become second nature.

Areas you want to change

Write down your resolutions and how you can go about keeping them. Anticipate any barriers to success and write out how you might deal with them. For example, your resolution might be to exercise twice a week but you might anticipate the barrier being lack of time to fit it into your daily life. So you could nip this in the bud by creating a schedule and making time to exercise, ensuring it becomes a priority. You may need to think hard about how to slot it in. Could that catch-up with your friend over a drink become a jog in the park or a yoga class together? Planning the potential pitfalls in advance means you'll be ready to bat them out of the park if they do come about.

I get a lot of feedback from the Princess Planning community about resolutions because many of them buy the planners as their first step on the road to change. So many tell me that when they are true to themselves, they set achievable goals that they have more success achieving. This means following what your heart is telling you and not what Mrs Gubbins next door is doing. Happiness looks different for us all and our path to get there will vary – so when it comes to making positive changes, listen to your inner voice and don't compare yourself to others.

It's not the destination, it's the journey

Creating good daily habits is just as important as setting goals, maybe even more so. When I was trying to lose weight, what stuck was making lasting little changes to my day-to-day eating routine. Once I did that, the goal was so much easier to achieve. The first habit I set about instilling was making my environment healthier with fewer calorific 'treats' – I stopped buying so much unhealthy food and instead stocked up on healthier alternatives, so that if I wanted to snack, then at least it could be on something that was diet-friendly. I knew I wouldn't be able to avoid the temptation of my favourite biscuits in the cupboard so I didn't buy any, which meant the whole family benefited from my healthier food habits. For me, the habit of picking at food throughout the day was really ingrained so it helped to make a swap first before stopping snacking completely.

When you are trying to replace old habits with new healthier ones, bringing in substitutes can be really helpful. For example:

* Introduce one healthy snack a day – try swapping your 3 p.m. biscuits for fruit.

* Instead of two glasses of wine, have one.

* Get off the bus three stops early and walk briskly to your destination.

The other micro-habit I have become evangelical about is (as you know by now!) writing down my food for the day and planning my meals. It's so ingrained now, it's like brushing my teeth – I never forget. Five minutes spent doing this prepares me for the day ahead.

Don't multitask

You didn't expect me to say that, did you? I've been banging on throughout the book about spinning plates every day and turning you into an organisational wizard, but when it comes to resolutions, I think we should keep it simple. Start with one change and once you've made sufficient headway with that, move on to your next resolution. It's tempting to jump onto the change bandwagon all guns blazing – you throw away all the tempting treats from your cupboard, banish the booze, buy a gym membership and for the first week, you're raring to go. Most people find it hard to effect long-term change this way, because when reality kicks in you often fall off the wagon completely.

I have always liked to set myself mini challenges to keep me going. When I was losing weight in the run-up to my wedding, I kept my overall goal in mind but what I found much more effective was working towards a weekly aim. I know that if I was only looking at the bigger picture goal, I'd have failed because it would have seemed so out of reach. Instead, celebrating the small wins gives a lovely boost.

Envisage your future self

If you could imagine yourself in six months or a year from now, having successfully fulfilled your resolutions, what would you and your life look like? Keep this vision in mind and it'll spur you on. When I was on my mission to boost my health and lose weight, it was the wedding that really motivated me. I'd imagine myself in my dream dress, surrounded by Nick, the children and all our family and friends. I wanted to be the best version of myself and for our loved ones to see how hard I'd worked to achieve that.

Looking ahead

This is something I like to do on my birthday as well as at the start of the year. Get out that pen and paper and list some experiences you want to try over the coming twelve months. It's a great way of putting yourself out there and trying something new. It could be taking a trip somewhere you've always wanted to go, learning to cook a new dish, reconnecting with an old school friend or dyeing your hair green. Go for it!

Enjoy it!

Embrace the fact that you are making a change or working towards something you want to achieve, whether that's learning Spanish or getting out of debt. Having a positive mindset is everything.

Think about the language you use when you talk to yourself. I used to say to myself things like, I wish I could lose the baby weight or I'm going to try to do X, Y or Z. It sounds a bit defeatist, doesn't it? How about swapping all those 'wishes' and 'wants' for 'wills' and 'cans'? I will stop smoking. I can get that promotion. I am going to save a little each month. The power of positive language is well documented and can go a long way to keeping you focused on your aim.

Staying on track

This isn't always easy, especially as during the first few days of the New Year we may be full of wide-eyed vigour, which gradually erodes as the more mundane routine of life begins again. If doing more exercise is your resolution, you may not feel like dragging yourself out of bed on a cold wintry morning to make that pre-work spin class.

There are several things I do to keep on top of my weight, even though it's been years since my big weight loss. Staying on track is as important to me now as it ever was – I don't want all that hard work I put in to be wasted and to have to start all over again. As you know by now, it's my meal planning and daily food diary that keep me on the straight and narrow and I have a weekly weigh-in on the scales too. I don't worry if I'm a few pounds heavier, it just means I rein it in a little over the week ahead.

Show up for yourself

Remember why you are making this change, and when that little devil appears on your shoulder to try to lead you astray, focus on the big-picture reasons for working towards your aim. Everything you want is within you to achieve – keep reminding yourself of your pledge to make the change and it'll help to keep you focused. You'll have some bad days and that's okay. Every mistake we make is a lesson for the future. Celebrate every achievement, no matter how small – not only do you deserve to pat yourself on the back, it'll help to keep you moving in the right direction.

Reach out to others

Surround yourself with good people who'll support your personal goals. If there are people in your life now who don't have your back, who undermine your ambitions or who snigger at your attempts, you may want to consider if they really deserve having you in their lives. We all need kind, caring, encouraging people and they are especially important at times like this.

Tell a supportive friend or family member about the resolution you are making and ask them to help to keep you motivated by checking in with you about progress every week. Making your aim public in this way can boost your determination.

Simple ways to make your life easier this year

I heard about a Japanese philosophy called kaizen, which is all about making continuous change for the better. It's not about big things but micro-changes, so that the nitty gritty of life flows better. I always like to think about this in January because any little systems we can implement in our day-to-day lives to claw back a bit of time have to be a good thing.

Here are some micro-changes you can bring into your life over the next week, regardless of whether it's January or June:

✳ Start a change pot using a large jar, jug or vase and stick in there any loose change you have at the end of each day that's under £1. You'll be thrilled at how much it adds up, especially if you leave it a whole year. It's practically free money!

✳ Put everyone's birthdays in your phone. Go on, stop putting it off.

✳ Keep stashes of birthday cards at home – have a crafternoon to get the kids making them in bulk and they'll last you all year.

✳ Compile up-to-date postal addresses on your phone so that you no longer scrabble around looking for Great-aunt Vera's details while trying to make the last post.

✳ Digitise your paperwork. If you have boxes of old bank statements, utilities contracts or employment documents clogging up desks and drawers, take photos of them and save them to the cloud. Shred the paperwork and free up some space at home. You can also do this for photographs and children's artwork.

✳ Gather up all the cables and chargers in your home and get rid of anything that's no longer in use. No doubt you'll find that charger from the Nokia you used ten years ago! Line a drawer with the inner tube from a kitchen roll, cut in half, and store cables tangle-free in each one.

✳ This sounds obvious but I can't tell you how many hours I've lost looking for my keys, phone or purse. If only I could reclaim that wasted time and use it to do something fun or relaxing. Keep these items and any others that you use constantly in the same place Every. Single. Day. Having a little basket or box for these items, for each member of the family, near the hallway will save your sanity.

You've got this

Planning the unplannable

Y ou can't plan for everything and you should be kind to yourself when things take a surprising turn. When a situation is out of your hands, it's overwhelming – whether that's because of a personal event or a global health crisis. It's important in those times to give yourself some space to reset.

Our framework and our routine might go out of the window for a while, but your planning toolkit will be ready and waiting to help you – step by step – to feel in control again amidst the chaos. When your world goes mad, each piece of planning is part of improving your own wellbeing.

Remember, making a plan is saying 'I can'!

Happy Planning!

The End

Be courageous.
The best is
yet to come

So, there you have it! I hope I have given you some planning principles that will see you through any event or milestone in life – even some that aren't covered in this book.
You now have a toolkit in your back pocket to get ahead of whatever life throws at you and hopefully you'll also enjoy the planning element as much as I do, rather than seeing it as a chore. And if that's a stretch, at the very least your newfound organisational wizardry will leave you with more time to do the things you love, whatever that may be. After all, this is not a rehearsal, we need to live our best lives right now. Thank you for coming on this planning journey with me, I am rooting for you.
Happy planning!

Love,

Charlotte xx

Acknowledgements

I'd like to start by thanking my husband Nick, who is my rock. This whole Princess Planning journey has been a rollercoaster. He has supported me from my mad initial idea to the big steps of taking on a premises and the biggest step of all – writing this book. He was my confidant, my chef and my early morning barista during the brainstorming sessions before work. He would constantly read through my scribbles and early drafts, he picked me up when I was down, and the writing of this book would never have been completed without him. He believed in me even when I had my own self-doubts!

My three children Lewis, Harriet and Reubin, who are as proud as they are shocked of what has happened to their mum in the last three-and-a-half years. They have been astonished at this remarkable journey as much as I have and I couldn't have done this without their love and support – they truly are my world!

I would like to thank the awesome team at Penguin Random House. The incredible Emma, who after my initial shock made me believe that I had an author within me, the team of Tamsin, Síofra, Michelle and Patsy, who gave me an incredible amount of support and made the writing of this book possible.

Finally, I would like to thank the Instagram community that has welcomed me in with open arms – they are my extended family. I have made amazing life friends and enjoy everything from the daily banter to helping and supporting people on their journeys. Without their continued backing the writing of this book, and the whole Princess Planning dream, would never have been possible.

Index

Use this space to make any extra notes!

....

....

....

....

....

....

....

....

....

....

....

....

....

....

....

....

....

....

Happy Planning

Shop my range of pretty stationery at
www.princessplanning.co.uk
You'll find organisers, trackers, meal
planners, food diaries and much more.

I love to see all the other planners out there so please share
your progress and pictures using #HappyPlanningBook

[Instagram] @princess.planning

3

Ebury Press, an imprint of Ebury Publishing
20 Vauxhall Bridge Road
London SW1V 2SA

Ebury Press is part of the Penguin Random House group of companies
whose addresses can be found at global.penguinrandomhouse.com

First published by Ebury Press in 2021

www.penguin.co.uk

A CIP catalogue record for this book is available from the British Library

ISBN 9781529107241

Design by Emily Voller

Illustrations by Sophie Martin

Printed and bound in Great Britain by Clays Ltd, Elcograf S.p.A.

The authorised representative in the EEA is Penguin Random House
Ireland, Morrison Chambers, 32 Nassau Street, Dublin D02 YH68.

Penguin Random House is committed to a
sustainable future for our business, our readers
and our planet. This book is made from Forest
Stewardship Council® certified paper.